The Gallup Polls
Of Attitudes
Toward Education
1969–1973

Edited by Stanley Elam
Editor, *Phi Delta Kappan*

Phi Delta Kappa

Graphic Design: William Tracy

Library of Congress Number 73-90469

Contents

Charles F. Kettering II, 1931-1971

This volume is dedicated to the memory of Charles F. Kettering II, for it was his idea that the Gallup polls of public attitudes toward education would be useful to educators who seek to improve the schools by making them serve the public better.

"Chuck" Kettering was the grandson of one of the great American automotive geniuses. He found his life work in striving to rectify inequities and indignities. Convinced early that education is a major instrument in social improvement, he was indefatigable in stimulating and guiding the educational projects of the Charles F. Kettering Foundation and of CFK Ltd., which he himself founded and chaired. Frequently, however, he would go beyond the reach of any institution to extend personal support and understanding. A certificated teacher in the state of Colorado, he was perhaps the most insightful of the committee members who helped George Gallup frame questions for the polls recorded herein.

Charles F. Kettering II was a man of courage, energy, enthusiasm, imagination, and devotion to the noblest goals of education. He has left a personal legacy that will not soon be forgotten.

Acknowledgements

The Gallup Polls, a three-volume work, was published in 1972 by Random House. It anthologizes nearly 36 years of the syndicated columns reporting survey results gathered by the Gallup organization. It does not include the annual Gallup polls of attitudes toward the public schools begun in 1969, when Charles F. Kettering II, board chairman, and Edward Brainard, president of CFK Ltd., made the happy decision to finance such a series. This volume anthologizes that five-year series.

The first Gallup education poll (1969) was published by CFK Ltd. and disseminated chiefly by the Institute for Development of Educational Activities, Inc., using its attractive newsletter, the I/D/E/A *Reporter.* Because of the *Reporter's* limited circulation, and because of an established relationship between CFK Ltd. and Phi Delta Kappa,* Mr. Kettering and Mr. Brainard suggested inclusion of the second poll in one of the fall issues of the *Phi Delta Kappan* in 1970. This would put the poll into the hands of 80,000 education leaders promptly (today the number is nearly 90,000), and ensure its availability in libraries throughout America. The editors welcomed the idea, of

---

*Phi Delta Kappa's Research Services Division was made possible by a Kettering Foundation grant of $70,000 in 1966. Mr. Kettering and Mr. Brainard were both members of the foundation's staff.

course, and the poll has become a September *Kappan* fixture. The sale of hundreds of thousands of reprints testifies to the value attached to it by the education community.

The poll's success is due primarily to the genius of George Gallup, who was provided a vehicle for expressing his lifelong interest in the schools. He has insisted every year on personally analyzing the data collected by his organization and preparing the published report. Even in 1972, when he was recovering from a painful accident, he met every deadline. Now Dr. Gallup has contributed the introductory chapter to this book. Phi Delta Kappa is grateful for his invaluable services.

A number of other people have made important contributions. Foremost among them, of course, were the late Mr. Kettering and Mr. Brainard, his friend and colleague at CFK Ltd. Mr. Kettering took a strong personal interest in the project and the questions asked over the first three years reflect his lively curiosity and his educational convictions. After Charles Kettering's untimely death late in 1971, the CFK Ltd. Board of Directors, chaired by Jean Kettering, Mr. Kettering's widow, voted to continue the poll as part of the CFK Ltd. program. Its continuation through 1974 is ensured, but in June of that year CFK Ltd. will be dissolved and a new source of financial support must be found if the project is not be be abandoned in 1975.

A special note of thanks is due Mr. Brainard, an educator and PDK member whose enthusiasm, organizational abilities, and fund of ideas were all essential to the poll's success.

A number of educators and interested laymen were called upon to discuss the trends and developments in education whose public impact is measured by these polls. Many of the questions came directly from the sessions attended by these men and women and by Mr. Kettering, Mr. Brainard, Dr. Gallup, Dr. Gallup's assistant, Rita Sappenfield, and myself. Persons included at one time or another in the planning sessions were Medill Bair, superintendent of schools, Hartford, Conn.; Forbes Bottomly, superintendent, Seattle schools; B. Frank Brown, Information and Services, I/D/E/A; Senator George L. Brown, Colorado Senate, and executive director, Metro Denver Urban Coalition; Senator Allen Dines, Colorado Senate;

Ernest Jones, acting superintendent of schools, St. Louis; Richard Koeppe, superintendent, Cherry Creek Schools, Englewood, Colo.; Carl L. Marburger, state commissioner of education, Trenton, N.J.; Gordon McAndrew, superintendent of schools, Gary, Ind.; Greta D. Murchison, principal, J. Hayden Johnson Junior High School, Washington, D.C.; Etta Lee Powell, principal, North Bethesda Junior High School, Bethesda, Md.; Thomas A. Shaheen, superintendent, San Francisco schools; Kenneth Schoonover, superintendent, Arapahoe County Schools, Littleton, Colo.; and Donald Waldrip, superintendent, Cincinnati schools. These talented and busy people gave freely of their time and energies.

The Board of Directors of CFK Ltd. deserve special thanks for approving the continuing polls project. They are B. Frank Brown, Senator George L. Brown, Jean S. Kettering (chairwoman), and Leo C. McKenna.

Having worked closely with her in the preparation of the polls for publication, I feel particularly grateful to Rita Sappenfield, assistant to Dr. Gallup, for her efficient handling of all the details of the series. The final chapter, reprinting *A Look Into Your School District,* is almost entirely her work. Graphics for that popular little volume, first printed in 1971 and frequently reprinted, were provided by C. William Wolfe. We are sorry that the format of this volume did not permit us to reuse them. Mrs. Sappenfield also compiled the index to this volume, another reason why we are deeply in her debt.

Stanley Elam
Editor, *Phi Delta Kappan*

November, 1973

Chapter 1
The First Five Years:
Trends and Observations*

The *raison d'etre* of these annual surveys sponsored by CFK Ltd. is to help guide the decisions of educators. Progress is only possible when the people are properly informed and when they are ready, through their tax dollars, to bear the costs of progress. For these reasons, these surveys are directed chiefly toward appraising the state of public knowledge and ascertaining public attitudes toward present practices, readiness to accept new programs, and ideas for meeting educational costs. In the performance of this work, we, too, sincerely hope that we are making a contribution to the field of education.

*   *   *

The public schools have passed through a trying period during the five years covered by the surveys reported in this book (1969-1973). The dominant mood of the nation during this period has been one of disillusionment brought about by the war in Vietnam, student protests, racial strife, and Watergate. Nevertheless, respect for and confidence in the public schools, this peculiarly American institution, remain at a high level.

*This summary of the first five polls of public attitudes toward education was written by Dr. Gallup in August, 1973, after the fifth poll was completed.

Education in the United States is still widely regarded as the royal road to success in life. At the same time, a few clouds are appearing on the horizon; unless those who are interested in the continued strength and well-being of the public schools heed these portents, public education in the nation could face a worrisome future.

Perhaps the best measure of the strength of these adverse forces is to be found in the failure of school bond issues to win majority acceptance in many school districts. Views of the public on matters relating to the financial needs of the public schools have been gauged from year to year in these CFK Ltd. surveys. During the five-year period there has been little change in the public's attitudes, with a majority taking a negative view about meeting the full financial requests of their local school boards.

The Public's Chief Concerns

The public harbors many concerns about the public schools. Chief among these is the lack of discipline. In all but one of the last five years, the nation's adults sampled in these surveys have named discipline as the number one problem of the schools in their own communities.

Court rulings defending student rights have not helped the discipline situation, although they have almost ended the *in loco parentis* principle, at least at the college level.

Another factor in the discipline situation is the state laws which compel young people to remain in school until the age of 17 or 18, even though some students are wholly uninterested in academic work and become troublemakers in the classroom. Since the public is reluctant to change these age requirements, it remains for school administrators and teachers to find better ways to motivate the uninterested students, or, failing this, to devise disciplinary measures that will be more effective than those presently utilized.

One obvious way to reach students who are not interested in academic subjects is to expand and give greater emphasis to career education programs. The public strongly supports this idea, as has been found in these surveys.

In fact, the public has responded favorably to proposals that students be permitted to spend their school time outside the school, learning what they can from local business or industry and fitting themselves for jobs in the community following high school graduation. Such plans have the double merit of removing malcontents from the classroom and placing them in training situations that offer an opportunity to become productive members of the community at an early age.

The importance of providing a different kind of education for those students who are most responsible for the discipline problems of the school cannot be underestimated. The many good things which the schools are achieving in every community seldom come to light in the local press. Student fights, vandalism, and turbulence in the classroom, on the other hand, are nearly always front-page news.

The unfavorable publicity which this discord generates is likely to have two consequences: It increases the difficulties of getting bond issues passed and, in many districts, leads to a flight from the public schools to the independent schools by children from the more affluent homes. It needs hardly to be added that parents who pay substantial sums for tuition in private schools are not likely to carry the flag to get school bonds passed, nor are those citizens who are distressed by the turmoil in the schools likely to go to the polls to cast a "yes" vote.

In short, while discipline is properly a responsibility of the home, the schools must perforce be more effective in mitigating this problem, or they will continue to suffer the consequences.

Another concern the American public has about the schools relates to the growing militancy of teachers. Teachers, like those in other callings, have a right to promote their economic interests and to have available an effective mechanism to express their grievances. Unionization offers a practical way to achieve these ends, and the public, generally, agrees that teachers should have the right to form unions. At the same time, a majority of the public is against permitting teachers to strike. This attitude may seem unrealistic to many; yet, unrealistic or not, it is a fact that must be taken into account.

During the last three decades the position of the teacher has changed, at least in the way the public regards this profession. In the 1930s and 1940s teachers were thought to be grossly underpaid public servants who engaged in teaching chiefly because of their dedication to education.

In the struggle to obtain parity with other professions, teachers have been compelled to adopt, in many situations, a militant position. This carries with it obvious dangers. If it means that teachers maneuver themselves into an adversary role *vis-á-vis* the public, then the public, which controls the purse-strings, has all the advantage.

A case in point is tenure, which is becoming an issue in many school districts. With the supply of teachers increasing relative to the demand, and with teacher salaries having improved during the sixties, the public understandably adopts an unfavorable attitude toward tenure, a fact found in answers to questions in the surveys that have dealt with this issue.

Likewise, the public looks favorably upon holding teachers and the schools accountable for the progress of students. This has not yet reached, nor is it likely to reach in the near future, a stage that would permit parents to sue if children of "normal intelligence" reached the sixth grade without being able to read. But it does show up in the public's desire to see how well their schools/students compare in test scores with schools/students in similar situations throughout the nation.

Insistence on accountability is likely to grow in the years ahead, judging from survey findings. This will take the form of trying to find valid ways to test educational performance. The argument presented in the past — that no two communities are exactly alike and therefore test results are not applicable — fails to reckon with the capabilities of computers that can adjust and equate for virtually all relevant factors, thus making it possible to arrive at meaningful comparisons.

The adverse factors in the public's thinking about the public schools need to be balanced against the favorable. Important among the latter is the public's receptiveness to new ideas and to change. In every community a few rock-ribbed individuals will fight any attempt to institute reforms or new programs, but the majority — too often inarticulate — generally approves any proposal for improving the educational program if the proposal sounds reasonable.

Some of the proposals that the public has supported in this series of surveys include:

- sex education in the schools,
- performance contracts,
- management experts to advise on costs/educational goals,
- year-around schools,
- nongraded schools,
- alternative schools.

The questionable success of some innovations that have enjoyed the enthusiastic support of educators and later have failed to live up to expectations — some reading and math programs, to cite two examples — will almost certainly provide those who oppose change with powerful arguments against any type of reform. Their arguments must be met with objective proof that has been lacking in the case of too many innovations in the past.

Racial integration must be considered one of the positive changes that have occurred in the schools in recent years. In many communities integration has been a disruptive issue and one of the most sensitive with which schools have had to deal. Survey findings offer some useful insights into public attitudes on this divisive question. Most important, perhaps, is the fact that where integration has taken place there is general acceptance of the situation and approval of the step. What has confused many writers and commentators is the distinction which the public makes between integration, the goal, and busing, a means to this end. Busing is widely disapproved, but this disapproval does not carry over to integration itself.

The flight by whites from the inner cities to the suburbs, we learned this year, is not primarily due to the desire of parents to take their children out of schools that are largely attended by blacks, but is for virtually the same reasons that people without school-age children wish to escape from the congestion and attendant ills of the big cities. At least this is what respondents told us.

A successful resolution of the problem of discipline would almost certainly bring a change in the attitudes of those parents who are moving to the suburbs chiefly to remove their children from inner-city schools.

Correcting Misapprehensions About the Schools

The schools of the nation have had a "poor press"

during the last five years. But since a properly organized information program can overcome the bad publicity which too often colors the public's thinking, there is the very real possibility that this situation can be changed.

Any survey that seeks to reveal the public's understanding of what the public schools are doing, or trying to do, will uncover a shocking lack of information, especially in the case of those individuals who do not have children presently attending the public schools. And since most of the opposition to bond issues comes from this sector of the public, it is imperative that the public schools give far more attention than they have to informing the general public.

The press is set up to report events, and the more traumatic are more likely to reach the front page. Usually the "good" news will go neglected unless school administrators themselves take the trouble to find it and see that it is dealt with in an interesting and informative manner. In fact, most newspapers welcome this kind of help, since few of them can afford to hire educational experts for their news staff and since few reporters spend the time it takes to dig up interesting articles. The costs to the school of providing this kind of information are entirely justifiable. Taxpayers have every right to know what they are getting for their money, especially in a time when educational costs are constantly increasing, and this cannot be achieved by neglecting to tell the positive side of what the schools are doing.

Making Parents Part of the Program

It seems obvious to me that the educational program of the nation must take into account more fully than it has in the past the home environment of the student. Any scientific assessment of student success is certain to reveal the important part played by the home in educational achievement. Historically, the schools have avoided making parents part of the teacher team, under the mistaken notion that teachers should not meddle in outside matters. Partly, this reluctance arises out of fear of parental criticism. Consequently, a wall has been built between the two, and contacts of a constructive order have been few and unavailing.

This situation must change if the school is to meet its

full responsibility for the education of the youth of the land. Parents must become an integral part of any educational program, and their instructional effort in the home must be seen as essential to the success of the child in school. Programs must be launched in every school district to educate parents and to see that they live up to their responsibilities. This step will not be as difficult to take as one may think. An earlier study, which we conducted under the aegis of the Charles F. Kettering Foundation, brought to light the noteworthy fact that most parents, even those with college educations, want help and guidance. Most parents are eager to learn what they can do in the home to help their children in school. After all, every parent wants his children to be successful in life. Obviously, not all parents can be expected to give up one evening a week or a month to learn what they should do at home to aid their children's progress in school, but the vast majority say they are willing to do so. If the programs for accomplishing this are really helpful, and if there is objective evidence to prove they are, then the educational system in the nation can, and should be, broadened to include the home as well as the school.

A properly conceived plan of helping parents do a more effective job of motivating their school-age children, organizing their homelife to enable them to do the best work in the classroom, and instructing them in the many areas not included in formal education offers, in my opinion, the greatest opportunity to reach higher educational standards and at the lowest cost.

Chapter 2
First Annual Survey:
How the Nation Views
The Public Schools

Purpose of the Study

The purpose of this survey, sponsored by CFK Ltd. and reported in the following pages, is to measure and record the attitudes of the American public toward the public schools in the year 1969. Benchmarks have been set to enable change to be measured in the years ahead.

The survey is national in scope and is based upon a representative sample of all adults. Results, it should be pointed out, do not apply to any single community, although they do provide a norm for comparison purposes.

Since attitudes and knowledge are closely related, many questions asked of respondents were included for the purpose of measuring the kind and amount of information possessed by representative citizens regarding their local schools.

An important objective of the study was to learn how typical citizens judge the quality of education in their local schools — the criteria they use in arriving at a judgment as to the excellence — or lack of it — in their local school system.

A realistic measure of the public's attitude toward their schools is the willingness of the people in a community to vote tax increases when there is need for greater financial assistance. A detailed analysis of the results obtained on this issue of taxes and financial aid is included in this report. Since school bond issues are being defeated with greater frequency across the nation, the survey results shed light on those groups in the nation most likely to support or to oppose bond issues calling for tax increases.

Other areas covered in the present survey deal with attitudes of the public toward teachers, the teaching profession, and toward their local school boards — the kinds of information the public would like to have regarding their local schools — the awareness of the public of school problems — and criticisms of school policies.

The study represents the joint planning of the staff of CFK Ltd. and the staff of Gallup International.

Research Procedure

The Sample. The sample embraced a total of 1,505 adults. It is described as a modified probability sample of the nation. A total of 327 interviewers took part in the survey; their work was done in every area of the country and in all types of communities, selected by random methods. These communities, taken together, represent a true microcosm of the nation.

The Interviewing Form. Questions included in the questionnaire were selected after many pretests were conducted in the Interviewing Center maintained by the Gallup organizations in Hopewell, New Jersey, and in a pilot study undertaken in 27 areas of the country.

Time of Interviewing. The field work for this study was conducted during the period of February 4 through February 20, 1969.

The State of Information About the Local Schools and Education

Judging by the answers to many questions included in this survey, the conclusion can be drawn that the public is only fairly well informed about the local schools and very poorly informed about education itself.

When adults comprising the sample of the general public were asked to give their own appraisal of the amount of their knowledge of the local schools, only about one in five (19%) replied, "quite a lot." At the other extreme more than four in ten (41%) frankly admitted that they know "very little."

Parents of children now attending the public schools were obviously better informed than those persons without children in the public schools, but even in this group of parents the percentage saying they know "quite a lot" about the local schools was not very impressive — 27%.

To measure the public's information about the schools, a series of test questions was included in the interviewing form. All persons in the survey were asked if they knew the names of their local school officials, with these results:

Percentage Who Knew Name Of

The local superintendent of schools	56%
The principal of the elementary school in your neighborhood	47%
The principal of the high school attended by children in your neighborhood	40%
The president of the local school board	26%

To gain insight into the extent of the public's knowledge in particular areas, questions requiring a higher level of knowledge were included. These asked about the shortage of classroom space, the percentage of dropouts in the local schools, the percentage of high school graduates going on to college, the costs to educate each child.

Those who reported that they "didn't know" provide evidence of the lack of information in these special areas, and an unwillingness even to make a guess.

	Don't Know
Is there a shortage of classroom space?	15%
Are there many high school dropouts?	30%
What percentage of high school graduates go on to college?	33%
What is the cost to educate a child per year in the local schools?	57%

It should be pointed out that the above table lists only those who said they "don't know" or were unwilling to make a guess. Those who did reply were not necessarily accurate in their replies.

Perhaps the most revealing question is one that asked each person to give his idea of a good school — to cite the "things that would make you decide that a school is a *good* school." Most of the information that the public possesses about the schools concerns the happenings — the news — reported in the newspapers or through other media. Knowledge about education itself is very limited, at least the kind of knowledge that has to do with the curriculum and goals of education. For example, when those in the survey were asked to tell how they would judge a school — the things that would make them decide that a school is a good school — their answers reveal a very low level of sophistication.

The criterion most often cited is "qualified teachers," but the replies reveal that there is little understanding of what is meant by a "qualified teacher." The few who go on to explain what they mean by this term usually describe the "qualified teacher" as one who is capable of interesting the children in their schoolwork or one who gets along well with parents.

Second in importance in judging a "good school," based upon the number of mentions, is "discipline." About one-third of all persons included in this survey said that this is a way to judge the quality of a school.

The third criterion most often cited is the physical equipment — modern school buildings and equipment.

Because of the frequently voiced criticism about the "frills" in public school education, a higher percentage of those interviewed might have been expected to cite this as a way to judge the schools. But this did not prove to be the case. While a few say they would judge a school on the basis of the emphasis given to the three Rs, even more say that a good school offers a wide variety of courses that are interesting to the students. And a total of 4% mention specifically a "good library."

When all the persons included in the survey were asked to tell in what respects the local schools are "not so good," their answers generally fall into these categories: "lack of discipline," "overcrowding of students," "poor transportation," "buildings too old," "integration," "no prayers." Some complain about "poor teaching or poor teachers," but on the whole there is rather little complaint about the local schools, especially the quality of education.

When asked specifically to name the "biggest problems with which the public schools in this community must deal," the greatest number of mentions go to "discipline." Second in order of mention is the lack of school facilities (buildings and equipment.) Third in order of mentions are answers dealing with teachers — shortages, lack of proper selection, etc. Fourth comes finances and fifth comes "integration and segregation."

Communication with the Public

To establish base points in order to make comparisons possible in the future — and to see just how much and what type of information about the public schools is now reaching the general public, including parents of school children — a series of questions was included in the interviewing form that deal with the different media and the kinds of information received and the kind of information that the public would like to have.

The first question in this series asked: "During the last year, have you received any newsletter, pamphlet, or any other material telling what the local schools are doing?"

A total of 35% of the entire sample answered yes to this question. When this figure is analyzed, a marked difference appears between those with no children and those with children in the public schools. In the case of those who have no children, only 16% say they have received such material from the schools, as opposed to 57% of those who do have children now attending the local public schools.

A majority of all persons (60%) report that they have read articles in the local newspapers during the last month about the local schools — with little difference in the figures between those with and those without children in the schools. A total of 36% say they have heard something about the local schools on radio during the last month, and a similar percentage (35%) say they have seen something on television about the schools in this same period of time.

Among the various media, the preferred source of information is the newspaper. Individuals in the cross-section were asked: "From your own personal viewpoint, what is the best source of information about the local schools?" As stated, local newspapers are cited most often, followed in turn by personal communication (children, neighbors, etc.), school officials and personnel, radio and/or television, meetings at the school (PTA, school programs, etc.), and school newsletters/pamphlets and publications.

Important for the school community is the fact that people say they would like to know more about the schools. When they were asked: "Would you like to know more about the schools in this community?" nearly two-thirds (65%) said yes. This finding agrees with other studies that have dealt with the public's interest in education. Significantly, even a majority of those without children express an interest in more information about the schools.

When asked specifically what kind of information they would like to have, the answers deal to a large extent with the courses taught — the curriculum — innovations being introduced and why — college requirements — and the like. Significantly, there is great interest in the very areas that most school publicity presently neglects — the content of courses and the educational process versus school operations.

The Major Complaints

The greatest complaint against the schools of the country, at the present time, is lack of discipline. This fact comes to light in many ways in this survey. Undoubtedly the present importance of discipline in the minds of the people is the result of the rash of disorders on the college campuses of the nation — and in some high schools. From a public relations viewpoint, this · criticism should be heeded — particularly by those school districts which are facing bond issues in the next year or two. Lack of proper discipline is often associated, as pointed out earlier, with "poor education." If school officials cannot keep students in line, then the school, in the eyes of the public, is a "poor" one.

To obtain the public's views on this issue, the following question was asked: "How do you feel about the discipline in the local schools — is it too strict, not strict enough, or just about right?"

Only 2% think it is "too strict" whereas 49% think it is "not strict enough." A total of 44% think it is "about right" with 5% having "no opinion." Parents with children in public school are inclined to be more satisfied with things as they are; 52% say discipline is "about right," 45% say it is "not strict enough," and 2% say it is "too strict."

Significantly, parents with children in parochial schools are the most critical of the public schools in the matter of discipline and cite as one advantage of the parochial schools (over the public schools) the better discipline maintained in the former.

Criticism of the schools in respect to discipline is greatest in the big cities of the nation, greater among Negroes than among whites, and greater among low income groups than among upper income groups.

Criticism of lack of discipline in the public schools extends to the failure to do more about the way boys and girls dress for school. When all those included in the survey were asked if they thought there should be "greater regulation of the way children dress for school, or less?" the replies show the following division:

Regulation of Dress

For greater regulation	53%
For less regulation	7%
All right at present	36%
No opinion	4%

Again, the replies show that the better educated are the least critical and of the major religious groups, Catholics are the most critical.

Attitudes Toward Teaching and Teachers

Probably no better measure of the public's high esteem for teaching and for schools could be found than parents' views toward teaching as a profession. When asked if they would like to have a child take up teaching in the public schools as a career, three out of every four say they would. And in the case of parents with children now in the public schools, the ratio is even higher — four out of five.

The weight of opinion is that teachers' salaries are too low. Although nearly half say they are "about right" and only 2% think they are "too high," one-third (33%) think they are too low.

On the question as to whether teachers should be given automatic raises, or whether these raises should be given to some and not to others, there is an equal division of opinion — 44% say yes; 45% say no; 11% have no opinion.

Of those with opinions, more favor permitting teachers to join unions than oppose this; but a substantial majority oppose giving teachers the right to strike.

Throughout the nation the public recognizes the difficulty of getting *good* teachers and holding them. Only a third of those reached in the survey say that in their own local schools there is no difficulty getting good teachers, and only a third say that there is no difficulty in keeping them.

Although there seems to be general satisfaction with the teachers, this should not be taken as approval of the entire teaching staff. The question of tenure was not asked specifically, but respondents were asked if some of the teachers in the local school system should be dropped. A total of 38% said yes; 22% said no; 40% had no opinion. The reasons most often given for dropping teachers were incompetence, personality problems, age problems — teachers too young or too old.

Attitudes Toward School Boards And Their Problems

Across the country school boards generally are thought to be doing a good job. More than three times as many respondents give them an "excellent" rating as give them a "poor" rating. And when asked specifically about their work, or aspects of it, the ratings are high. In only one important respect is their work questioned. When asked if the school board in their local community is politically motivated — if local politics play a part in the decisions made by the school board — more answer yes than answer no.

The generally high regard in which school boards are held is reflected in the question put to each individual in the survey: "If some one asked you to be a school board member, would you be interested?"

Nearly one person in three (31%) said he would, if asked. Analysis of the data shows that more men than women would like to serve (35% to 29%). Of those who have had the advantage of a college education, nearly half say they would be interested; in the professional and business group 41% say they would be interested; and interest in becoming a school board member is highest in the youngest age group — those ages 21 to 30. In this group 52% say they would be interested.

The fact that these respondents say they would be interested does not mean that they will volunteer, or go through an expensive and time-consuming political campaign to be elected. If these practices could be removed, there would be no dearth of qualified men and women to serve on the school boards of the nation.

To gain further insight into local school problems, as the public sees them, each person in the survey was asked what changes in the school system he would favor if he were to become a school board member.

Nearly three-fourths of those who have children in the public schools made specific suggestions. These concern chiefly the professional staff, the course content or curriculum, and the buildings and facilities. The category getting the next largest number of suggestions was "discipline."

This suggestion, discipline, comes up particularly high with parents of children in parochial schools.

Local school boards are thought by 69% of the respondents to work hard to "improve the quality of education." Nearly as many (62%) say the school board "works hard to see that the schools function efficiently and at the lowest cost." The greatest criticism is leveled at the cost of school buildings. A total of 40% think they are more expensive than they need to be.

Citizen Participation

In another survey of the adult population, it was found

that most citizens think that the school buildings should be used for community purposes as well as for students.* In most towns and cities this policy is followed. To find out just how many persons had made use of school facilities, this question was asked: "Have you attended any lecture, any meeting, or any social occasion in any local school building during the last year?"

Nearly six in 10 (59%) of the respondents who now have children in the public or parochial schools of the community have. Only one person in six (17%) of those without children in school answer yes to this question.

On the other hand, rather few have *ever* attended a meeting of the local school board. In the entire group only 16% say they have *ever* attended a school board meeting.

Slightly more than half (52%) of the parents of children in the local schools say they belong to the PTA or to a similar group. A higher percentage (65%) of those with children in parochial schools say they belong to such a group.

Whereas more than half of the parents of children in the public schools say they belong to some kind of parents' group, fewer than half of this group say they attend regularly. When those who do not attend regularly were asked to tell why they did not go more often, most cited such things as "no one to care for the children," "conflict with other commitments," and similar reasons. Some say that not much gets accomplished — "it is a waste of time."

Persons who do not belong to parents' groups, even though they have children in the schools, gave somewhat similar reasons for not joining. About one in 10 said there was no PTA, or similar organization, in his community. Others say they have only recently moved into the community — more say they are not "joiners."

Financial Support

The best measure of the attitudes of the general public toward the public school system in America is its readiness to support the schools financially — to vote for an increase in taxes if the schools need more money.

*C. F. Kettering Foundation Survey by Gallup International, *Parent's Reactions to Educational Innovations,* May, 1966.

Obviously the situation varies from community to community across the nation; an infinite variety of financial problems exist and there is an infinite variety of ideas as to how best to deal with them.

Many efforts were made to find a question wording which 1) would measure general attitudes applicable to most situations, and 2) could be repeated from year to year to measure change in attitudes. Obviously the ideal question would show a high correlation with known facts — the proportion of communities voting in favor or against school bond issues. In this sense, it could be predictive.

With these requirements in mind, the question that was finally used on the interviewing form is worded as follows:

Suppose the local public schools said they needed much more money. As you feel at this time, would you vote to raise taxes for this purpose, or would you vote against raising taxes for this purpose?

Analysis of the vote recorded on this question reveals the groups or segments of society in which support of the public schools is greatest and least. Those who are involved in school bond campaigns may find this information useful, although it should be pointed out again that no two local situations in the nation are exactly alike. But the chances are great that in any given community the attitudes of the various groups will not depart too greatly from the national norm.

Those who analyze the results of school bond issues must always take account of the low voter turnout in the typical school bond election. One fact is clear — those who bother to vote are *not* typical of those who do not vote. The situation is not unlike that found in elections for political office in the United States. In presidential races only slightly over 60% of the population of voting age will take the trouble to register and vote. In school bond elections the percentage tends to be far less. Fortunately for the schools, the nonvoters in these elections tend to be more negative in their attitudes than those who do vote, judging from the data obtained in this study.

For example, in answer to the question about voting more funds for the local school, as stated above, the vote in favor is 45%; against, 49%; and 6% are in the "don't know" category. If only those who say they voted in the last school bond election are used as the base, the vote for and against is almost exactly even.

A look at the vote by groups is most revealing.

Level of education reached turns out to be an important factor. In fact, on the basis of the major breakdowns provided in this study, it is the most important factor. The better educated are more inclined to vote favorably on school bond issues than the less well educated. Below are the votes on the question:

Suppose the local public schools said they needed much more money. As you feel at this time, would you vote to raise taxes for this purpose, or would you vote against raising taxes for this purpose?

Vote by Level of Education

	For %	Against %	No Answer or Don't Know %
College graduate	61	34	5
College incomplete	54	43	3
Technical, trade, business school	52	47	1
High school graduate	44	50	6
High school incomplete	41	54	5
Grade school or less	33	59	8

Although it could be argued that it is the lower income, lower educated persons who have the most to gain, it is the better educated who understand best the value of an education and, at the same time, are the ones who become most involved in the local schools — the ones who take the most active part in school affairs.

Since education and income are closely related, it is to be expected that those in the highest income brackets are more in favor of voting for taxes to help the schools than those in the lower income levels. Results by income levels show the following:

Vote by Income Levels

Annual Family Income	For %	Against %	No Answer or Don't Know %
$15,000 and over	55	41	4
$10,000 to $14,999	49	47	4
$7,000 to $9,999	46	48	6
$5,000 to $6,999	47	50	3
$4,000 to $4,999	41	53	6
$3,000 to $3,999	42	48	10
Under $3,000	33	59	8

Vote by Age Levels

	For %	Against %	No Answer or Don't Know %
21 to 29 years	56	39	5
30 to 49 years	47	48	5
50 and over	39	55	6

It should be noted that the younger age groups are better educated than the older groups. The percentage of those who have attended college is highest in the 21 to 29 group and lower in each older age group.

It is to be expected that parents with children in the public schools would vote more favorably on school financial requests than those who have no children in the schools or have children in the parochial schools. Here are the figures:

Children in the Schools

	For %	Against %	No Answer or Don't Know %
Parents of children now attending public schools	51	44	5
Parents of children now attending parochial schools	40	56	4
Adults with no children in school	41	53	6

As a group, Protestants are more in favor than Catholics. When all Protestants are compared with all Catholics —

both those with and without children in school — the following results are obtained:

	For %	Against %	No Answer or Don't Know %
Protestants	47	47	6
Roman Catholics	41	55	4

Observations and Conclusions

Three of the major tasks of the public school system in the United States can be stated as follows: first, to interest a greater number of citizens in the public schools; second, to increase financial support as needs grow; third, to create a climate in the community and in the schools favorable to an improvement in the quality of education.

In a sense, and as the data from this survey show, all of these problems tend to be interrelated. When the survey results dealing with the many aspects of education embraced in this survey are examined, these conclusions seem warranted:

1. While the American people seem reasonably well-informed about school activities, they are ill-informed about education itself.

2. Since they have little or no basis for judging the quality of education in their local schools, pressures are obviously absent for improving the quality.

3. Fortunately, the public would like more information about modern education — the new methods being tried and new ideas about the kind of education that is needed. In short, they need and ask for the kind of information that is presently not provided by the various media of communication.

4. From a public relations viewpoint, the biggest problem at the present time for the schools is the matter of discipline. This is the greatest criticism the public makes of the schools and the school officials. Those who have no children complain the loudest, but even those with children in the public schools criticize school officials and personnel for not being more strict in the matter of deportment and dress of students. As long as this complaint about the

public schools is present, the vote on school bond issues is likely to suffer accordingly.

5. The teaching profession probably has never been held in higher esteem in this nation. This is complimentary to those who are in the profession — but the urge to get into this field, on the part of so many students today, may create another problem in another decade or two.

6. The public has accepted the right of teachers to join unions. But the public has not yet accepted the right of teachers to strike, and, judging from the data, many reject the idea of tenure, at least until better ways are found for weeding out incompetent teachers.

7. The weight of opinion is that public school teachers are underpaid. But this situation is changing and the number holding such an opinion is far less than it was a decade ago.

8. School boards get a high vote of approval across the nation. The public believes they work hard to improve the quality of education and to run the schools efficiently. At the same time, some believe that their decisions are often politically motivated.

9. There is no dearth of individuals who would be interested in becoming school board members. But, as other studies have shown, most do not want to fight their way through political campaigns, requiring a lot of time and money, in order to serve the public in this capacity.

10. The public schools do a reasonably good job of interesting parents in school affairs. They do a very poor job in reaching those who do not have children attending the schools. A better way must be found to reach those persons in the community who do not happen to have children in the public schools, so that these persons may become informed, involved, and active. The future of the schools to a great extent depends on success in achieving this goal.

11. If willingness to vote additional taxes for schools saying they need more money is accepted as a good test of the public's attitudes toward the public schools, then the nation divides itself about evenly. This does not mean that one-half of the nation is opposed to the public schools. It means simply that approximately half would resist requests for more money — and presumably vote against new bond issues.

12. An important factor that works in favor of getting school bond issues accepted is the simple fact that those groups or segments of society that are opposed are those least likely to cast their ballots in these elections. The best-educated tend to be most favorable and most likely to vote; the least well-educated make up the group least favorable but, at the same time, least likely to vote. This observation holds only for the nation as a whole. This does not mean that in some situations the opposite may not be true.

13. Finally, the survey helps to explain the slowness of the schools to accept innovations. So much effort is consumed in keeping the schools operating and doing a reasonably good job that little time can be devoted by school officials in promoting change. The public is so uninformed about innovations and so lacking in objective ways of judging school achievement that little, if any, pressure is exerted by them to make improvements, or is likely to be exerted until they are more knowledgeable in this area.

The State of Information About the Local Schools and Education

How much do you know about the local schools, quite a lot, some, or very little?

	National Totals %	No Children In Schools %	Public School Parents %	Parochial School Parents %
Quite a lot	18	12	27	21
Some	40	30	50	50
Very little	42	58	23	29
	100	100	100	100

Do you happen to know the name of the superintendent of schools?

	National Totals %	No Children In Schools %	Public School Parents %	Parochial School Parents %
Yes	56	46	68	58
No	44	54	32	42
	100	100	100	100

Do you happen to know the name of the principal of the elementary school in your neighborhood?

	National Totals %	No Children In Schools %	Public School Parents %	Parochial School Parents %
Yes	47	24	76	47
No	53	76	24	53
	100	100	100	100

Do you know the name of the principal of the high school attended by the children in your neighborhood?

	National Totals %	No Children In Schools %	Public School Parents %	Parochial School Parents %
Yes	40	26	58	35
No	60	74	42	65
	100	100	100	100

Now, a few questions about the local school board. First, do you happen to know the name of the president of the board?

	National Totals %	No Children In Schools %	Public School Parents %	Parochial School Parents %
Yes	26	21	32	28
No	72	76	67	72
No answer	2	3	1	--
	100	100	100	100

Do you think there is a shortage of classroom space in this community?

	National Totals %	No Children In Schools %	Public School Parents %	Parochial School Parents %
Yes	56	49	65	51
No	29	29	29	35
Don't know/ no answer	15	22	6	14
	100	100	100	100

What is your guess as to the cost per child per year in the public schools of your community?

	National Totals %	No Children In Schools %	Public School Parents %	Parochial School Parents %
Gave a $ figure	43	40	45	54
Don't know	57	60	55	46
	100	100	100	100

Are there many high school dropouts in this community?

	National Totals %	No Children In Schools %	Public School Parents %	Parochial School Parents %
Quite a few	26	24	28	24
Almost none	41	36	46	44
Don't know	30	37	22	27
Commented: average, even one is too many, etc.	3	3	4	5
	100	100	100	100

What percentage of the high school graduates from your high school go on to college, do you think?

	National Totals %	No Children In Schools %	Public School Parents %	Parochial School Parents %
Gave an actual % figure	67	65	70	75
Don't know	33	35	30	25
	100	100	100	100

What do you think are the biggest problems with which the public schools in this community must deal?

	National Totals %	No Children In Schools %	Public School Parents %	Parochial School Parents %
Discipline	26	27	24	39

Facilities	22	17	27	26
Teachers	17	14	20	24
Finances	14	15	15	7
Integration/ segregation	13	15	12	8
Parents lack of interest	7	7	7	5
Transportation	5	5	5	5
Curriculum	4	3	5	9
Pupils lack of interest	3	4	3	4
Miscellaneous	8	7	8	5
There are no problems	4	3	6	1
Don't know/ no answer	13	17	9	13
	136*	134*	141*	146*

*Totals exceed 100% because some respondents gave more than one answer.

Have you read any book in the last year that deals with education?

	National Totals %	No Children In Schools %	Public School Parents %	Parochial School Parents %
Yes	16	15	17	19
No	84	85	83	81
	100	100	100	100

What is the name of the book(s)?

	National Totals %	No Children In Schools %	Public School Parents %	Parochial School Parents %
1 title given	4	4	5	4
2 titles given	2	2	2	--
3 titles given	--	--	--	2
4-6 titles given	1	--	1	--
No titles given	10	9	10	12
	17*	15*	18*	18*

*Equals percent of persons reading any book dealing with education during the last year.

Communication with the Public

During the last year, have you received any newsletter, pamphlet, or any other material telling what the local schools are doing?

	National Totals %	No Children In Schools %	Public School Parents %	Parochial School Parents %
Yes	35	16	57	44
No	61	81	39	52
Can't recall	4	3	4	4
	100	100	100	100

During the last month have you read any articles in the newspapers about local schools?

	National Totals %	No Children In Schools %	Public School Parents %	Parochial School Parents %
Yes	60	54	65	77
No	34	39	29	17
Can't recall	6	7	6	6
	100	100	100	100

Have you heard anything about local schools on radio during this period?

	National Totals %	No Children In Schools %	Public School Parents %	Parochial School Parents %
Yes	36	32	39	46
No	58	61	55	51
Can't recall	6	7	6	3
	100	100	100	100

How about television?

	National Totals %	No Children In Schools %	Public School Parents %	Parochial School Parents %
Yes	35	33	36	53
No	59	61	59	43
Can't recall	6	6	5	4
	100	100	100	100

From your own personal viewpoint, what is the best source of information about the local schools?

	National Totals %	No Children In Schools %	Public School Parents %	Parochial School Parents %
Local newspaper	38	41	34	46
Word of mouth: own children, students, neighbors	25	21	31	15
School personnel	20	17	23	16
Radio & TV	16	19	11	18
Meetings at school	15	11	20	19
School publications	8	5	12	11
Don't know/ no answer	6	9	2	3
	123*	123*	135*	126*

*Totals exceed 100% because some respondents gave more than one answer.

Would you like to know more about the schools in this community?

	National Totals %	No Children In Schools %	Public School Parents %	Parochial School Parents %
Yes	65	55	77	74
No	35	45	23	26
	100	100	100	100

Same question, answers by other categories.

	Yes %	No %	Don't Know/ No Answer %
Sex			
Men	65	34	1
Women	66	34	*
Race			
White	64	35	1
Nonwhite	76	24	--

(Continued on next page)

Education

Elementary grades	54	46	--
High school incomplete	66	34	*
High school complete	67	33	--
Technical, trade, or business school	77	22	1
College incomplete	75	24	1
College graduate	62	37	1

Occupation

Business and professional	68	32	--
Clerical and sales	67	33	--
Farm	67	33	--
Skilled labor	70	30	--
Unskilled labor	73	26	1
Non-labor force	45	54	1

Age

21 to 29 years	75	24	1
30 to 49 years	73	27	--
50 years and over	51	48	1

Religion

Protestant	67	33	--
Roman Catholic	66	34	--
Jewish	47	51	2
All others	59	41	--

Region

East	62	37	1
Midwest	67	33	--
South	69	30	1
West	63	37	--

Income

$15,000 and over	63	36	1
$10,000 to $14,999	73	27	--
$ 7,000 to $ 9,999	68	31	1
$ 5,000 to $ 6,999	68	31	1
$ 4,000 to $ 4,999	73	27	--
$ 3,000 to $ 3,999	54	45	1
$ 2,500 to $ 2,999	51	49	--
Under $2,499	45	54	1

Community size

500,000 and over	59	41	*
50,000 to 499,999	69	31	*
25,000 to 49,999	74	26	--
Under 25,000	68	31	1

*Less than 1%

The Major Complaints

How do you feel about the discipline in the local schools — is it too strict, not strict enough, or just about right?

	National Totals %	No Children In Schools %	Public School Parents %	Parochial School Parents %
Too strict	2	2	2	--
Not strict enough	49	52	45	58
Just about right	44	39	52	36
Don't know/ no answer	5	7	1	6
	100	100	100	100

Same question, answers by other categories.

	Too Strict %	Not Strict Enough %	Just About Right %	Don't know/ No Answer %
Sex				
Men	1	54	40	5
Women	2	45	47	6
Race				
White	2	47	46	5
Nonwhite	1	69	29	1
Education				
Elementary grades	*	53	41	6
High school incomplete	2	52	43	3
High school complete	2	50	43	5
Technical, trade or business school	1	45	48	6
College incomplete	1	54	40	5
College graduate	1	36	54	9
Occupation				
Business and professional	1	42	50	7
Clerical and sales	1	48	46	5
Farm	4	42	53	1
Skilled labor	*	53	44	3
Unskilled labor	2	54	39	5
Non-labor force	1	55	37	7

(Continued on next page)

Age

21 to 29 years	4	45	44	7
30 to 49 years	1	49	46	4
50 years and over	1	52	41	6

Religion

Protestant	1	49	46	4
Roman Catholic	1	50	44	5
Jewish	--	58	33	9
All others	7	46	32	15

Region

East	1	51	42	6
Midwest	2	47	46	5
South	1	47	47	5
West	2	55	38	5

Income

$15,000 and over	1	46	48	5
$10,000 to $14,999	1	46	48	5
$ 7,000 to $ 9,999	3	50	43	4
$ 5,000 to $ 6,999	1	49	43	7
$ 4,000 to $ 4,999	1	57	40	2
$ 3,000 to $ 3,999	4	46	48	2
$ 2,500 to $ 2,999	--	51	42	7
Under 2,499	2	56	33	9

Community Size

500,000 and over	2	61	32	5
50,000 to 499,999	1	55	38	6
25,000 to 49,999	5	46	49	--
Under 25,000	2	37	56	5

*Less than 1%.

Some people feel the schools do not go far enough in regulating the way boys and girls dress for school. Do you think there should be greater regulation of the way children dress for school, or less?

	National Totals %	No Children In Schools %	Public School Parents %	Parochial School Parents %
Greater	53	55	50	63
Less	7	7	5	4
All right as it is	36	31	42	32
No opinion	4	7	3	1
	100	100	100	100

Same question, answers by other categories.

	Greater %	Less %	All Right As Is %	Don't Know/ No Answer %
Sex				
Men	54	6	35	5
Women	53	7	36	4
Race				
White	53	7	36	4
Nonwhite	54	6	33	7
Education				
Elementary grades	58	3	31	8
High school incomplete	60	5	29	6
High school complete	53	5	39	3
Technical, trade, or business school	60	3	37	--
College incomplete	47	11	38	4
College graduate	43	12	42	3
Occupation				
Business and professional	50	10	37	3
Clerical and sales	51	10	36	3
Farm	36	3	60	1
Skilled labor	56	4	34	6
Unskilled labor	58	5	31	6
Non-labor force	55	7	34	4
Age				
21 to 29 years	44	18	34	4
30 to 49 years	53	4	39	4
50 years and over	58	4	33	5
Religion				
Protestant	53	6	36	5
Roman Catholic	60	4	33	3
Jewish	42	14	42	2
All others	34	22	40	4
Region				
East	53	6	35	6
Midwest	49	7	41	3
South	55	6	34	5
West	58	7	31	4
Income				
$15,000 and over	49	9	36	6
$10,000 to $14,999	51	8	39	2
$ 7,000 to $ 9,999	51	5	41	3
$ 5,000 to $ 6,999	53	6	35	7

(Continued on next page)

$ 4,000 to $ 4,999	68	3	23	6
$ 3,000 to $ 3,999	58	8	32	2
$ 2,500 to $ 2,999	45	6	47	2
Under $2,499	57	9	25	9
Community size				
500,000 and over	55	7	32	6
50,000 to 499,999	56	6	33	5
25,000 to 49,999	54	5	41	--
Under 25,000	50	6	40	4

Attitudes Toward Teaching and Teachers

Would you like to have a child of yours take
up teaching in the public schools as a career?

	National Totals %	No Children In Schools %	Public School Parents %	Parochial School Parents %
Yes	75	69	81	78
No	15	18	12	14
Don't know/ no answer	10	13	7	8
	100	100	100	100

Same question, answers by other categories.

	Yes %	No %	Don't Know/ No Answer %
Sex			
Men	71	17	12
Women	78	14	8
Race			
White	74	16	10
Nonwhite	75	15	10
Education			
Elementary grades	75	14	11
High school incomplete	72	18	10
High school complete	73	15	12
Technical, trade, or business school	71	16	13
College incomplete	78	16	6
College graduate	80	13	7

Occupation			
Business and professional	75	15	10
Clerical and sales	76	18	6
Farm	83	16	1
Skilled labor	73	14	13
Unskilled labor	75	12	13
Non-labor force	72	18	10
Age			
21 to 29 years	65	18	17
30 to 49 years	77	14	9
50 years and over	75	16	9
Religion			
Protestant	76	14	10
Roman Catholic	76	14	10
Jewish	63	30	7
All others	59	22	19
Region			
East	73	17	10
Midwest	76	13	11
South	73	16	11
West	78	15	7
Income			
$15,000 and over	82	11	7
$10,000 to $14,999	74	17	9
$ 7,000 to $ 9,999	74	16	10
$ 5,000 to $ 6,999	74	13	13
$ 4,000 to $ 4,999	83	10	7
$ 3,000 to $ 3,999	71	12	17
$ 2,500 to $ 2,999	60	29	11
Under $2,499	69	19	12
Community size			
500,000 and over	71	17	12
50,000 to 499,999	73	18	9
25,000 to 49,999	82	13	5
Under 25,000	78	13	9

Do you think salaries in this community for the teachers are too high, too low, or just about right?

	National Totals %	No Children In Schools %	Public School Parents %	Parochial School Parents %
Too high	2	3	2	2
Too low	33	30	35	27
Just about right	43	43	44	47
Don't know/ no answer	22	24	19	24
	100	100	100	100

Do you think teachers should be given automatic raises or should raises be given to some and not to others?

	National Totals %	No Children In Schools %	Public School Parents %	Parochial School Parents %
Yes, automatic	44	45	45	32
No, not automatic	45	43	47	51
No opinion	11	12	8	17
	100	100	100	100

How do you feel about teachers joining labor unions?

	National Totals %	No Children In Schools %	Public School Parents %	Parochial School Parents %
Those Who Are In Agreement				
Yes	23	22	24	33
Yes, if they want to do so	12	11	13	4
Yes, for bargaining power	7	7	7	8
Yes, their own union	3	3	3	--
Yes, if conditions justify	--	--	-	4
	45	43	47	49
Those Who Are Against				
No	33	33	33	33
No, it is a profession	5	6	4	8
No, they are public servants	1	2	--	--
No, this would only give them power to strike	1	*	1	2
	40	41	38	43
No opinion	3	3	3	3
Miscellaneous	1	2	1	*
Don't know/ no answer	11	11	11	5
	15	16	15	8
Totals	100	100	100	100

*Less than 1%

Note: Questions asked earlier this year through the Gallup Poll find a higher proportion of respondents in favor of permitting teachers to join labor unions. The question was worded differently, which may account for the difference. Both, however, show majorities in favor.

Do you think teachers should have the right to strike?

	National Totals %	No Children In Schools %	Public School Parents %	Parochial School Parents %
Those Who Say "Yes"				
Yes	19	19	19	19
Yes, if conditions justify	10	11	11	10
Yes, it is their right	8	7	8	6
	37	37	38	35
Those Who Say "No"				
No	38	37	36	39
No, it hurts the children	11	11	11	10
No, public servants should find another way	8	7	8	11
No, it sets a poor example	2	2	2	2
	59	57	57	62
Don't know/ no answer	4	6	5	3
Totals	100	100	100	100

Note: Questions asked earlier this year through the Gallup Poll show almost exactly the same results on the question of the right of teachers to strike.

Do you think this local public school system has a hard time getting good teachers?

	National Totals %	No Children In School %	Public School Parents %	Parochial School Parents %
Yes	52	49	54	51
No	32	31	34	34
Don't know/ no answer	16	20	12	15
	100	100	100	100

Do you think this local public school system has a hard time keeping good teachers?

	National Totals %	No Children In Schools %	Public School Parents %	Parochial School Parents %
Yes	48	46	49	48
No	35	31	40	34
Don't know/ no answer	17	23	11	18
	100	100	100	100

Do you think there are some teachers in the local public school system who should be dropped or fired? If "yes," why?

	National Totals %	No Children In Schools %	Public School Parents %	Parochial School Parents %
Yes	38	32	45	39
No	22	19	27	15
Don't know/ no answer	40	49	28	46
	100	100	100	100

Reasons Why

Incompetent	21	19	24	24
Personality problems	9	7	11	6
Too young/ too old	5	3	7	4
Lack of communi- cation with children	3	2	4	4
Miscellaneous	1	1	2	2
Don't know/ no answer	3	3	3	4
	42*	35*	51*	44*

*Exceeds total replying "yes" because some respondents gave more than one answer.

From what you know, are teachers in your community pretty well satisfied with their pay and working conditions or are they dissatisfied?

	National Totals %	No Children In Schools %	Public School Parents %	Parochial School Parents %
Satisfied	35	32	39	33
Dissatisfied	35	35	35	35
Don't know/ no answer	30	33	26	32
	100	100	100	100

Are teachers in this community paid more money, or less money, than teachers in other comparable communities?

	National Totals %	No Children In Schools %	Public School Parents %	Parochial School Parents %
More	12	11	12	14
Less	17	16	20	11
About same	34	34	35	36
Don't know/ no answer	37	39	33	39
	100	100	100	100

Attitudes Toward School Boards and Their Problems

How good a job do you think the school board does?

	National Totals %	No Children In Schools %	Public School Parents %	Parochial School Parents %
Excellent	25	22	29	25
Above average	16	14	19	12
Fair	21	20	22	17
Poor, terrible	7	6	9	7
Don't know/ no answer	31	38	21	39
	100	100	100	100

Do you think it is politically motivated?
That is, do local politics play a part in decisions
made by the board?

	National Totals %	No Children In Schools %	Public School Parents %	Parochial School Parents %
Yes	44	43	44	46
No	39	35	44	33
Don't know/ no answer	17	22	12	21
	100	100	100	100

If someone asked you to be a school board
member, would you be interested?

	National Totals %	No Children In Schools %	Public School Parents %	Parochial School Parents %
Yes	31	27	35	39
No	67	71	64	58
Don't know/ no answer	2	2	1	3
	100	100	100	100

Why do you say that?

	National Totals %	No Children In Schools %	Public School Parents %	Parochial School Parents %
Those Who Say "Yes"				
Interested in helping	27	24	29	32
Am qualified	4	3	1	5
	31	27	30	37
Those Who Say "No"				
Not qualified	31	33	30	20
Don't have time necessary	15	9	22	25
Not interested	9	11	6	7
Have no children in school	9	17	*	3

*Less than 1%

Too much respon-sibility	6	5	7	1
	70	75	65	56
No answer	5	5	5	7
Totals	106*	107*	100	100

*Totals exceed 100% because some respondents gave more than one answer.

If someone asked you to be a school board member, would you be interested?

	Yes %	No %	Don't Know/ No Answer %
Sex			
Men	34	64	2
Women	29	70	1
Race			
White	30	69	1
Nonwhite	40	56	4
Education			
Elementary grades	13	82	2
High school incomplete	26	73	1
High school complete	28	71	1
Technical, trade, or business school	40	59	1
College incomplete	51	47	2
College graduate	44	55	1
Occupation			
Business and professional	41	58	1
Clerical and sales	36	62	2
Farm	17	82	1
Skilled labor	29	69	2
Unskilled labor	29	69	2
Non-labor force	21	78	1
Age			
21 to 29 years	52	47	1
30 to 49 years	32	66	2
50 years and over	20	78	2
Religion			
Protestant	30	68	2
Roman Catholic	34	64	2
Jewish	28	70	2
All others	37	63	--

(Continued on next page)

Region

East	32	66	2
Midwest	32	67	1
South	31	68	1
West	31	67	2

Income

$15,000 and over	37	62	1
$10,000 to $14,999	41	58	1
$ 7,000 to $ 9,999	33	65	2
$ 5,000 to $ 6,999	27	72	1
$ 4,000 to $ 4,999	28	70	2
$ 3,000 to $ 3,999	21	76	3
$ 2,500 to $ 2,999	22	73	5
Under 2,499	21	78	1

Community size

500,000 and over	32	67	1
50,000 to 499,999	33	65	2
25,000 to 49,999	28	69	3
Under 25,000	30	69	1

If you were to become a school board member, what changes in the schools would you favor?

	National Totals %	No Children In Schools %	Public School Parents %	Parochial School Parents %
Curriculum, courses, course content	15	14	16	19
Professional staff	14	11	20	13
Building & facilities	11	8	15	10
Better discipline	9	9	9	11
Financial	4	5	4	4
Transportation	3	2	4	5
Segregation/ integration	2	2	1	2
Miscellaneous	2	2	3	5
	60	53	72	69
I'd make no changes; it's all right as is	11	10	12	7

Don't know/ no answer	44	50	36	40
Totals	115*	113*	120*	116*

*Totals exceed 100% as some respondents gave more than one reply.

Does it work hard to improve the quality of education?

	National Totals %	No Children In Schools %	Public School Parents %	Parochial School Parents %
Yes	69	63	77	63
No	11	10	12	16
Don't know/ no answer	20	27	11	21
	100	100	100	100

Does it work hard to see that schools function efficiently and at the lowest cost?

	National Totals %	No Children In Schools %	Public School Parents %	Parochial School Parents %
Yes	62	56	70	58
No	15	15	15	19
Don't know/ no answer	23	29	15	23
	100	100	100	100

Do you think that school buildings are more expensive than they need to be?

	National Totals %	No Children In Schools %	Public School Parents %	Parochial School Parents %
Yes, in general	26	27	23	33
Yes, too fancy, too elaborate	14	13	13	18

(Continued on next page)

(Continued from preceding page)

No, in general	42	40	47	34
No, they are not good enough	7	7	7	4
Don't know/ no answer	11	13	10	11
	100	100	100	100

Do you think money is spent foolishly by the school authorities or the local school board?

	National Totals %	No Children In Schools %	Public School Parents %	Parochial School Parents %
Yes	26	26	25	31
No	65	62	70	61
Don't know/ no answer	9	12	5	8
	100	100	100	100

Citizen Participation

Have you attended any lecture, any meeting, or any social occasion in any local school building during the last year?

	National Totals %	No Children In Schools %	Public School Parents %	Parochial School Parents %
Yes	37	17	59	56
No	59	77	41	43
No answer	4	6	--	1
	100	100	100	100

Same question, answers by other categories.

	Yes %	No %	Don't Know/ No Answer %
Sex			
Men	33	63	4
Women	40	57	3

Race			
White	37	60	3
Nonwhite	33	60	7
Education			
Elementary grades	14	83	3
High school incomplete	28	68	4
High school complete	39	57	4
Technical, trade, or business school	40	58	2
College incomplete	51	44	5
College graduate	57	42	1
Occupation			
Business and professional	51	47	2
Clerical and sales	38	58	4
Farm	53	43	4
Skilled labor	37	60	3
Unskilled labor	31	64	5
Non-labor force	13	82	5
Age			
21 to 29 years	33	60	7
30 to 49 years	50	49	1
50 years and over	22	72	6
Religion			
Protestant	37	59	4
Roman Catholic	39	59	2
Jewish	23	75	2
All others	37	63	--
Region			
East	33	64	3
Midwest	42	54	4
South	33	63	4
West	44	53	3
Income			
$15,000 and over	50	46	4
$10,000 to $14,999	53	44	3
$ 7,000 to $ 9,999	40	58	2
$ 5,000 to $ 6,999	34	61	5
$ 4,000 to $ 4,999	25	71	4
$ 3,000 to $ 3,999	16	81	3
$ 2,500 to $ 2,999	16	75	9
Under $2,499	11	85	4
Community size			
500,000 and over	34	64	2
50,000 to 499,999	33	61	6
25,000 to 49,999	44	56	--
Under 25,000	40	56	4

Have you *ever* attended a school board meeting?

	National Totals %	No Children In Schools %	Public School Parents %	Parochial School Parents %
Yes	16	14	18	15
No	81	82	81	83
No answer	3	4	1	2
	100	100	100	100

Do you belong to the PTA or a similar group?

	Public School Parents	Parochial School Parents
Yes	52	65
No	48	35
	100	100

If "no": Since you do have children in school, what are your reasons for not belonging to the PTA or a similar group?

No time	21	11
Not interested	11	10
No PTA or similar group	9	10
New in this area	2	1
Health prevents attending	2	--
Miscellaneous	1	3
Don't know/no answer	2	--
	48*	35*

*Total equals number who do not belong.

If 'belong to PTA': Do you attend meetings regularly during the school year, or not?

Regularly	22	36
Not regularly	30	28
No answer	--	1
	52*	65*

*Equals percent of those belonging to PTA.

If "not regularly": Will you please tell why you do not regularly attend?

	Public School Parents %	Parochial School Parents %
No time	20	18
Not interested	6	5
Health prevents attending	1	1
Miscellaneous	3	1
Don't know/no answer	1	3
	30*	28*

*Equals percent of those not regularly attending PTA.

Financial Support

Suppose the local public schools said they needed much more money. As you feel at this time, would you vote to raise taxes for this purpose, or would you vote against raising taxes for this purpose?

	National Totals %	No Children In Schools %	Public School Parents %	Parochial School Parents %
For	45	41	51	40
Against	49	53	44	56
Don't know/ no answer	6	6	5	4
	100	100	100	100

Same question, answers by other categories.

	For %	Against %	Don't Know/ No Answer %
Sex			
Men	47	48	5
Women	43	50	7

(Continued on next page)

Race

White	46	49	5
Nonwhite	45	47	8

Education

Elementary grades	32	60	8
High school incomplete	41	54	5
High school complete	44	50	6
Technical, trade, or business school	52	47	1
College incomplete	54	43	3
College graduate	61	34	5

Occupation

Business and professional	56	40	4
Clerical and sales	44	52	4
Farm	31	62	7
Skilled labor	46	47	7
Unskilled labor	39	56	5
Non-labor force	41	53	6

Age

21 to 29 years	56	39	5
30 to 49 years	47	48	5
50 years and over	39	55	6

Religion

Protestant	47	47	6
Roman Catholic	41	55	4
Jewish	47	51	2
All others	48	44	8

Region

East	47	48	5
Midwest	40	54	6
South	50	44	6
West	43	51	6

Income

$15,000 and over	55	41	4
$10,000 to $14,999	49	47	4
$ 7,000 to $ 9,999	46	48	6
$ 5,000 to $ 6,999	47	50	3
$ 4,000 to $ 4,999	41	52	7
$ 3,000 to $ 3,999	42	48	10
$ 2,500 to $ 2,999	38	53	9
Under 2,499	32	61	7

Community size

500,000 and over	45	51	4
50,000 to 499,999	47	46	7
25,000 to 49,999	31	64	5
Under 25,000	46	48	6

Did you happen to vote in the last school bond election?

	National Totals %	No Children In Schools %	Public School Parents %	Parochial School Parents %
Yes	41	36	45	49
No	49	55	44	40
Can't recall	10	9	11	11
	100	100	100	100

Can you recall how you voted? Did you vote for or against the bond?

For	**26**	**21**	**33**	**22**
Against	10	11	8	15
Can't recall	5	4	4	12
	41*	36*	45*	49*

*Total equals percent of respondents voting in last school bond election.

Some people say that the federal government should pay all of the cost of a college education. Others believe that most of the costs should continue to be paid, as now, by parents and students. Which would you favor?

	National Totals %	No Children In Schools %	Public School Parents %	Parochial School Parents %
Federal government pay	16	15	17	12
Parents & students pay	70	71	69	70
Federal government & parents/students	7	8	7	9
Other methods	4	3	4	4
Don't know/no answer	3	3	3	5
	100	100	100	100

Composition of the Sample

Analysis of Respondents

	National Totals	No Children In Schools	Public School Parents	Parochial School Parents
Base figures	1,505	756	656	114
Percent of total	100%	50%	44%*	7*

*Total exceeds 50% because some parents have children attending more than one kind of school.

Analysis of Number of Children Attending Schools Whose Parents Are Respondents

Total Number of Children Attending Elementary And Secondary Schools 1,578

Number attending public schools	1,319
Number attending parochial schools	228
Number attending private day schools	20
Number attending private boarding schools	3
Number attending nursery schools, day-care centers, Head Start, etc.	8

Respondents are:

Sex	Raw Figure	%
Men	748	50
Women	757	50
	1,505	100
Race		
Whites	1,343	89
Nonwhites	149	10
Others	13	1
	1,505	100

Could you tell me the kind of business or industry the chief wage earner (head of household) in your immediate family works in and the kind of work he does there?

	Raw Figure	%
Business and professional	409	27
Clerical and sales	168	11
Farm	70	5
Skilled labor	270	18
Unskilled labor	312	21
Non-labor force	243	16
Undesignated	33	2
	1,505	100

What was the last grade or class you completed in school?

Elementary grades	262	18
High school incomplete	269	18
High school complete	471	31
Technical, trade or business school	88	6
College incomplete	200	13
College graduate	215	14
	1,505	100

Did you attend the schools in the community in which you now live?

Yes	478	32
No	1,018	68
No answer	9	--
	1,505	100

And what is your age, please?

21 to 29 years	263	18
30 to 49 years	674	45
50 years and over	562	37
Undesignated	6	*
	1,505	100

*Less than 1%

What is your religious preference — Protestant, Roman Catholic, or Jewish?

Protestant	1,014	67
Roman Catholic	380	25

(Continued on next page)

	Raw Figure	%
Jewish	57	4
All others	54	4
	1,505	100

(Show card 'X', side 1) Would you please give me the letter of the group which best represents the total annual income, before taxes, of all of the members of your immediate family living in your household?

	Raw Figure	%
$15,000 and over	195	13
$10,000 to $14,999	291	19
$ 7,000 to $ 9,999	374	25
$ 5,000 to $ 6,999	220	15
$ 4,000 to $ 4,999	122	8
$ 3,000 to $ 3,999	83	6
$ 2,500 to $ 2,999	55	4
Under $2,499	139	8
Undesignated	26	2
	1,505	100

Note: Each of the Gallup surveys includes a section titled "Design of the Sample." Because these sections are almost identical in each survey, only the most recent is included in this compilation. It appears at the end of Chapter 6.

Chapter 3
Second Annual Survey
Of the Public's Attitudes
Toward the Public Schools

Purpose of the Study

The purpose of the survey reported in the following pages is to measure and record the attitudes of the American public toward the public schools in the year 1970. Benchmarks have been set to enable change to be measured in the years ahead. Also, some questions have been asked that were asked in the 1969 survey in order to see if any changes have occurred within the year.

The survey is national in scope and is based upon a representative sample of all adults. Results, it should be pointed out, do not apply to any single community, although they do provide a norm for comparison purposes.

As in our 1969 survey, we are pointing out that a realistic measure of the public's attitude toward their schools is the willingness of the people in a community to vote tax increases when there is need for greater financial assistance. A detailed analysis of the results obtained on a series of questions dealing with taxes and financial aid to public and parochial schools is included in this report. Since school bond issues are being defeated with greater frequency across the nation, the survey results shed light on those groups in the nation most likely to support and to oppose bond issues calling for greater tax increases.

Other areas covered in this survey deal with attitudes of the public toward holding educators accountable for the progress of students, toward giving students a voice in school policies and procedures, toward sex education in the schools, and toward change and innovation.

This study represents the joint planning of the staff of CFK Ltd. and the staff of Gallup International.

Research Procedure

The Sample. The sample embraced a total of 1,592 adults. It is described as a modified probability sample of the nation. The work was done in every area of the country and in all types of communities, selected by random methods. These communities, taken together, represent a true microcosm of the nation. A full description of the adult sample will be found at the end of this report.

The sample also included a total of 299 students. These were boys and girls, one from almost every community included in the adult sample, who were enrolled in either the junior or senior classes in high school in April, 1970. Demographic information about these students appears in the section of the report entitled "Composition of the Sample."

The Interviewing Form. Questions included in the adult questionnaire were selected after many pretests were conducted in the Interviewing Center maintained by the Gallup organizations in Hopewell, New Jersey. Questions included in the high school student questionnaire were selected from the adult questionnaire, where applicable. When questions on the adult questionnaire were not applicable to the students, questions appearing on questionaires previously administered to college freshmen in another survey were used.

Time of Interviewing. The field work for this study was conducted during the period of April 15 through 20, 1970.

Observations and Conclusions

The 1970 survey of the public's attitudes toward the public schools, in addition to covering many areas not embraced in the 1969 study, offers some important clues to the future.

People continue to have a high regard for the schools of their community and they believe firmly that education is the royal road to success in America. Yet there is undeniably a new mood in the nation with which educators must reckon.

Student protests, both at the high school and college level, have, in the case of the curricula, opened the whole issue of whether education in America is reality-related. Students as well as adults are beginning to question the judgment of educators — the experts.

Budgets and bond issues are being voted down in increasing number. Evidence of this trend is to be found in the results of the present study. The U.S. Office of Education reports that in the last year (fiscal 1969) school bond issues were voted down by voters at a record rate. By dollar value, voters approved less than 44% of the $3.9 billion in bond issues put to the electorate. The $1.7 billion that passed comprised the lowest total since 1962. A decade ago 80% of such bond issues were approved.

The costs of education, as is true of everything else, increase constantly, and it is perhaps inevitable that as these costs mount, taxpayers are likely to become increasingly critical of educational policies.

When people read or hear about the lack of discipline in the schoolrooms of their own community — and the inability of administrators to cope with these and other problems — they see their tax money being wasted and the whole purpose of the schools perverted.

Few citizens take the time and trouble to inquire into the causes of these difficulties, or to appraise objectively the merits of the case from the educators' point of view. The end result, consequently, is likely to be another vote cast against the new bond issue or next year's budget.

Up to this point in history, the majority of citizens have been quite willing to take the word of the school board and of the teachers and administrators that the schools are doing a good job. They have looked with pride on the community's school buildings and its winning football or basketball teams. These have been good enough to convince many that the local schools are good. But evidence in the present study indicates that this way of judging the quality of education may be in for a change.

Most would like to have more objective data on student

achievement. In fact, the proportion who would like to have national tests administered in the local schools as a way to measure student progress and achievement and to compare progress with other schools is at a high level, as reported in this study.

One other fact needs to be pointed out. More than half of all parents of children in the schools today have had the advantage of some high school or college education. They can fall back on their own educational experience as a way to judge the progress of their children, something that was not possible a generation or two ago.

The well-educated parent is pro-education. He is the one most likely to vote in a school election, and he is most likely to vote yes on financial issues. Yet he is also likely to be more critical of school policies and the achievement or lack of achievement shown by his own children.

The public has an appetite for more information about the schools and what they are doing or trying to do. If the schools hope to avoid financial difficulties in the years ahead, they need to give far greater attention to this task of informing the public. And it isn't simply a matter of "selling" present policies. Public relations is a two-way street. It is important to tell the public about the schools, but it is also incumbent upon the schools to listen to the public's views and after serious examination take steps to meet just criticisms.

The Public Names the Biggest Problem Facing the Public Schools

The public again, in 1970, cites discipline as the greatest problem of the schools in their own communities. Next in order of mention come the problems of integration/segregation (busing), the problem of getting financial support for the schools, "good" teachers, and improving school buildings and facilities. The use of drugs and dope by students is mentioned often enough to place this relatively new problem in sixth place.

When those interviewed are asked specifically about discipline, only 2% say that discipline is "too strict." Slightly more than half (53%) say that discipline is "not strict enough." Another 31% say it is "just about right" and the remainder (14%) say they "do not know."

During the year the percentage of those saying that discipline is "not strict enough" has climbed four points. Parents of children enrolled in public schools are evenly divided between saying that discipline is "not strict enough" and that it is "just about right." Persons who have no children in school and parents of students enrolled in parochial schools are of the belief that discipline is not strict enough in the public schools. Negro parents are even more critical of the public schools on the point of discipline.

Surprisingly, more students say that discipline is "not strict enough" than say it is "too strict." The majority (60%) say that discipline is "just about right."

Who should assume more responsibility for correcting this situation?

When those who say that discipline is "not strict enough" are asked this question, a plurality of the adults say "the school" — teachers, administrators, or the school board. Slightly fewer adults say the parents should assume more responsibility. When the same question is put to the high school juniors and seniors who say that discipline is "not strict enough," the majority hold the teachers and school administrators responsible — not the parents.

In the report on discipline which was included in the first annual audit of education in 1969, it was pointed out that overall attitudes toward the schools are likely to be prejudiced by what the public believes is too much laxity or permissiveness in matters of discipline.

Parents are even more in favor of spanking than are teachers. When the National Education Association Research Division surveyed classroom teachers recently, it was found that 57% favor spanking. When parents of public school students were interviewed in this Second Annual Survey, 66% were in favor of spanking. A total of 29% disapproved, 5% had "no opinion." The issue of corporal punishment is becoming more widely discussed chiefly because of the lack of discipline and the increased disruption of the classrooms by students. Every one of the 50 states, with the exception of New Jersey, permits corporal punishment, although many schools have banned the practice. In many communities teachers have insisted on spanking rights in order to maintain discipline.

Teacher and Administrator Accountability

With the cost of maintaining the public schools rising year by year, the public's demand for some kind of measurement of student progress is certain to grow. There are obviously many factors that cannot be taken fully into account in the rating of schools. However, the argument that communities differ so greatly and that the home environment of students varies so much that comparisons are impossible can be answered to a large extent by present research techniques which permit the matching of samples. The computer can overcome many of the earlier problems of comparing one community with another and one school system with another.

Included in the interviewing form in the present survey were several questions designed to approach the subject of accountability in various ways.

The first question asked:

Would you like to see the students in the local schools be given national tests so that their educational achievement could be compared with students in other communities?

The adult public approves this idea. In fact, the vote on this question was 75% in favor, 16% opposed.

Another question presented the issue of greater accountability more directly:

Would you favor or oppose a system that would hold teachers and administrators more accountable for the progress of students?

The result was very much the same. A total of 67% of the adults voted in favor, 21% opposed the idea, and the remaining 12% had "no opinion."

Going one step further, another question asked:

Should each teacher be paid on the basis of the quality of his work or should all teachers be paid on a standard scale basis?

This question, of course, assumes that "quality of work" of a teacher can be determined in an objective manner — which many doubt. The principle of paying anyone on a standard basis — and overlooking his individual effort and success — runs counter to the prevailing ethos of the nation, especially in occupations that are regarded as professional. The results of this question indicate that adults regard teachers as they do other professional groups — 58% believe teachers should be paid on the "quality of work" and 36% believe teachers should be paid on a "standard scale basis."

A question about "tenure" probed this same area. The question asked was designed chiefly to gauge reactions to the general principle of tenure:

> Many states have "tenure" laws, which means that a teacher cannot be fired except by some kind of court procedure. Are you for giving teachers tenure or are you against tenure?

In reply to this question, 35% of the adults said they favored tenure laws, 53% opposed them.

In recent years, teacher organizations have become active in their own interest in many cities and sections of the nation. The adult public was asked this question:

> Have teacher organizations gained too much power over their own salaries and working conditions?

The response throughout the nation was 26% yes, 53% no.

Student Power

Parents and high school juniors and seniors hold widely differing views on the role students should play in determining such matters as curriculum, teachers, school rules, and school dress. Most parents, in each instance, believe that students "should not have more say" about what goes on within the school. Students, on the other hand, believe they should. The nearest the two groups come to agreeing is in the case of teachers — but even there the spread is 31 percentage points in their views.

The differences are revealed in the following results:

Should high school students have more say about what goes on within the school on matters such as curriculum? teachers? school rules? student dress?

	Yes %	No %	No Opinion %
Curriculum?			
Parents of children in public schools	40	55	5
High school juniors and seniors	83	15	2
Teachers?			
Parents of children in public schools	22	74	4
High school juniors and seniors	53	43	4
School Rules?			
Parents of children in public schools	38	58	4
High school juniors and seniors	77	22	1
Student Dress?			
Parents of children in public schools	40	56	4
High school juniors and seniors	76	23	1

Also, in the matter of awareness of student protests, a wide difference is found between students and parents. When asked if there have been any student protests in the schools during the present year (that is, between September, 1969, and April, 1970) nearly four in 10 of the students interviewed said yes, whereas only two in 10 of parents said there had been such protests.

Financial Support for the Public Schools

Opposition to voting more taxes for the local public schools increased during the year. This, of course, must be interpreted against a background of many developments in the economy — higher real estate taxes, inflation, and a greater struggle on the part of most families to make ends meet.

How to obtain adequate financial support is perhaps the most serious problem of the public schools in the United States, and a problem that needs more attention on the part of school administrators and school board members.

Persons in the lowest income and education levels are found to be most opposed to meeting new financial needs. On the other hand, these are the persons least likely to get to the polls on election day. Even so, opposition to paying more taxes for the schools is apparently growing even among those who normally could be expected to vote on this issue.

The vote by age levels, by level of education, and by those who have children in the public schools as opposed to those who do not, is instructive.

Suppose the local *public* schools said they needed much more money. As you feel at this time, would you vote to raise taxes for this purpose, or would you vote against raising taxes for this purpose?

	For %	Against %	No Opinion %
Age of Respondents			
21 - 29 years	44	49	7
30 - 49 years	40	56	4
50 years and over	32	60	8
Education of Respondents			
Elementary grades	28	63	9
High school incomplete	33	60	7
High school complete	33	61	6
Technical, trade, or business school	48	48	4
College incomplete	47	48	5
College graduate	61	33	6
Children in School			
Public school parents	43	54	3
Parochial school parents	37	58	5
No children in school	35	57	8

A majority of those questioned across the nation would like to transfer some of the burden of supporting the local schools from local real estate taxes to the state government. Whether this attitude springs from a genuine concern for the property owner or from the belief that respondents, as taxpayers, have to pay less if the state pays more is not apparent in the data. The vote in favor of asking the state government to bear a greater share of local school expenses is 54% to 34%.

In the poorer communities, where education costs per child are likely to be almost as great as in the richer communities, the shift would come as welcome and needed relief. It appears then, that the long-term trend is likely to be in the direction of lessening the burden on real estate to provide for the financial needs of the public school system.

Tax Aid for Parochial Schools

A hotly debated issue in many states is the extent to which parochial schools should be given financial aid by government sources. The Supreme Court has still to rule on important aspects of this issue. But at the present time, the public is willing to give favorable consideration to those who claim that such financial aid is needed to help the parochial schools make ends meet.

The question asked:

It has been proposed that some government tax money be used to help parochial schools make ends meet. How do you feel about this? Do you favor or oppose giving some government tax money to help parochial schools?

The vote on this issue was fairly close, with 48% in favor of giving some government tax money to parochial schools and 44% opposed.

When the vote is analyzed by groups, it is seen that parents of children in the public schools are evenly divided; parochial school parents are understandably in favor — but not to the extent that one might expect.

The Allotment (Voucher) System

Some nations follow a plan of alloting a certain sum of

money for the education of each child. The parents can then decide whether to send the child to a public, a private, or a parochial school. This proposal, now referred to in the United States as the "voucher plan," will actually be tried experimentally during the next few years in test communities, according to present plans.

Sentiment is rather evenly divided on adopting this proposal here in the United States, with a slight majority opposed. The national figures last spring were 46% opposed, 43% in favor. Parents of children in the public schools opposed by a vote of 49 to 41; those whose children were enrolled in parochial schools favored this plan by a vote of 48 to 40.

The vote was close enough to give real concern to those who believe the voucher plan carries with it a real threat to the quality of public school education.

Sex Education in the Schools

By an overwhelming majority, parents expressed their approval of sex education in the public schools. The vote of parents was 72% in favor to 22% opposed. Lowest approval was found among those who had no children of school age, yet even in this group the favorable vote was two to one.

In the opinion of a majority of parents with children enrolled in the public schools, sex education should include a discussion of birth control. The vote in favor was nearly two to one — actually 60% to 32%.

The same liberal viewpoint came to light in the results of a question which asked if married girls who attend high school and who are pregnant should be permitted to attend. In the case of parents, the vote was 49% in favor to 46% opposed. For all groups, including those who did not have children in school, the vote was almost a standoff — 46% in favor, 47% opposed.

The same three questions were put to high school juniors and seniors. Predictably, they were even more liberal in their views than were their parents. A total of 89% favored sex education courses; 82% approved of discussions of birth control; and 57% believed married pregnant high school girls should be permitted to attend classes.

Use of Drugs

The American public has become aware of a serious drug problem in their own public schools.

Even in the less densely populated areas of the country, there is increasing recognition of drug usage among school children. The figures for different areas of the country and for different sizes of communities are instructive.

Marijuana and other drugs are increasingly being used by students. Do you think it is a serious problem in your public schools?

	Yes %	No %	Don't Know %
Area of Country			
East	69	19	12
Midwest	55	28	17
South	60	25	15
West	78	12	10
Size of Community			
500,000 and over	77	11	12
50,000 - 499,999	76	11	13
25,000 - 49,999	75	10	15
Under 25,000	48	36	16

Interestingly, students differed somewhat with their parents as to the seriousness of the problem in their own schools. While two out of three adults (actually 64%) said the problem is serious, only 39% of high school juniors and seniors agreed.

There was not much conviction on the part of either adults or students that the schools are "doing a good job of teaching the bad effects of drug use." In the case of adults, the number who said the schools are not doing a good job, or have no opinion, adds up to 61%.

High school juniors and seniors were about evenly divided on this issue, 49% saying the schools are doing a good job of teaching the bad effects of drugs, 45% saying they are not.

Change and Innovation

Students were far more critical of the curriculum than

were their parents. A clear majority of high school juniors and seniors believed that the school curriculum in their own community "needs to be changed to meet today's needs." Parents by almost the same percentage said the curriculum is all right as it is. Stated in percentages, the students by a vote of 58 to 40 said the curriculum needs to be changed; their parents by a vote of 59 to 33 said it is satisfactory as it is.

The same generation gap came to light on a question which dealt specifically with innovation. Forty-three percent of students interviewed expressed the opinion that "the local public schools are not interested enough in trying new ways and methods," while only 19% believed that the local schools are "too ready to try new ideas." In the case of parents of public school children the vote was nearly even, 20% saying the schools are not interested enough in trying new ideas, 21% saying they are "too ready." The remainder had no opinion or said that the schools, in respect to trying new ideas, are "just about right."

Year-Around Schools

The question of keeping the schools open the year around to utilize school buildings and facilities to the full extent did not receive majority support either on the part of parents or of high school students. Yet it should be pointed out that, with educational costs mounting yearly, there is an important part of the population who do believe this idea has merit.

The favorable vote on this idea last April was rather considerable. A total of 42% of all adults favored it; 50% opposed; 9% had no opinion.

Rather surprisingly, 40% of the students themselves liked the idea; 58% opposed it.

In an earlier study, it was found that many parents oppose the idea of year-around schools chiefly because they believe such a change would interfere with their own vacation plans. With more and more parents taking winter vacations — or choosing some time of the year other than July and August — opposition to this plan can be expected to decline, especially if it can be substantiated that real economies will ensue.

The Major Problems

What do you think are the biggest problems with which the public schools in this community must deal?

	National Totals %	No Children In School %	Public School Parents %	Parochial School Parents %	High School Juniors & Seniors %
Discipline	18	18	18	20	17
Integration/ segregation	17	19	14	14	21
Finances	17	14	20	23	12
Teachers	12	11	15	12	21
Facilities	11	8	14	11	24
Dope/drugs	11	10	12	12	13
Curriculum	6	5	8	4	11
Parents' lack of interest	3	3	3	3	1
Transportation	2	3	2	2	3
School board policies	2	2	3	1	--
School administration	1	†	2	1	3
Pupils' lack of interest	†	†	1	2	5
Miscellaneous	3	3	3	2	8
There are no problems	5	3	7	5	2
Don't know/ no answer	18	21	11	18	5
	126*	120*	133*	130*	146*

†Less than 1%.
*Totals exceed 100% because some respondents gave more than one answer.

How do you feel about the discipline in the local public schools — is it too strict, not strict enough, or just about right?

	National Totals %	No Children In School %	Public School Parents %	Parochial School Parents %	High School Juniors & Seniors %
Too strict	2	2	2	2	15
Not strict enough	53	57	48	50	23

Just about right	31	21	47	37	60
Don't know/ no answer	14	20	3	11	2
	100	100	100	100	100

Same question, answers by other categories.

	Too Strict %	Not Strict Enough %	Just About Right %	Don't Know/ No Answer %
Sex				
Men	2	54	31	13
Women	2	52	31	15
Race				
White	2	52	32	14
Nonwhite	4	62	21	13
Education				
Elementary grades	1	55	28	16
High school incomplete	2	56	32	10
High school complete	2	50	35	13
Technical, trade, or business school	1	62	16	21
College incomplete	3	55	26	16
College graduate	2	47	39	12
Occupation				
Business and professional	1	52	32	15
Clerical and sales	3	52	34	11
Farm	3	42	51	4
Skilled labor	2	54	31	13
Unskilled labor	3	57	30	10
Non-labor force	†	53	24	23
Age				
21 to 29 years	4	41	35	20
30 to 49 years	2	51	38	9
50 years and over	†	61	24	15
Religion				
Protestant	2	53	33	12
Roman Catholic	2	56	27	15
Jewish	--	54	25	21
All others	3	44	31	22
Region				
East	2	54	28	16
Midwest	†	58	31	11
South	3	48	36	13
West	1	52	29	18

(Continued on next page)

Income

$15,000 and over	†	47	40	13
$10,000 to $14,999	2	58	27	13
$ 7,000 to $ 9,999	2	52	34	12
$ 5,000 to $ 6,999	1	56	30	13
$ 4,000 to $ 4,999	3	47	36	14
$ 3,000 to $ 3,999	--	54	37	9
Under $2,999	3	51	21	25

Community size

500,000 and over	1	61	23	15
50,000 to 499,999	1	58	26	15
25,00 to 49,999	--	70	22	8
Under 25,000	3	44	40	13

†Less than 1%.

If [discipline] "not strict enough," ask: Who should assume more responsibility for correcting this situation?

	National Totals	No Children In School	Public School Parents	Parochial School Parents	High School Juniors & Seniors
	%	%	%	%	%
Teachers	16	16	16	17	12
School administration	16	17	16	12	7
Parents	30	33	24	29	4
School board	6	6	5	8	2
Students	2	2	2	3	5
Others	2	3	1	†	--
Don't know	2	2	†	2	1
	74*	79*	64*	71*	31*

†Less than 1%.

*Totals exceed percentage replying "not strict enough" in previous questions because some respondents gave more than one answer.

Spanking and similar forms of physical punishment are permitted in the lower grades of some schools for children who do not respond to other forms of discipline. Do you approve or disapprove of this practice?

	National Totals	No Children In School	Public School Parents	Parochial School Parents	High School Juniors & Seniors
	%	%	%	%	%
Approve	62	60	66	66	40
Disapprove	33	34	29	31	56
No opinion	5	6	5	3	4
	100	100	100	100	100

Marijuana and other drugs are increasingly being used by students. Do you think it is a serious problem in your public schools?

	National Totals	No Children In School	Public School Parents	Parochial School Parents	High School Juniors & Seniors
	%	%	%	%	%
Yes	64	69	56	69	39
No	22	16	31	18	59
Don't know	14	15	13	13	2
	100	100	100	100	100

Do you feel that the local public schools are doing a good job of teaching the bad effects of drug use?

	National Totals	No Children In School	Public School Parents	Parochial School Parents	High School Juniors & Seniors
	%	%	%	%	%
Yes	39	34	47	39	49
No	25	26	24	24	45
Don't know	36	40	29	37	6
	100	100	100	100	100

Have there been any demonstrations protesting school policies or procedures in your public schools during this present school year?

	National Totals	No Children In School	Public School Parents	Parochial School Parents	High School Juniors & Seniors
	%	%	%	%	%
Yes	19	18	19	18	39
No	64	56	75	74	59
Don't know	17	26	6	8	2
	100	100	100	100	100

Teacher and Administrator Accountability

Would you like to see the students in the local schools be given national tests so that their educational achievement could be compared with students in other communities?

	National Totals	No Children In School	Public School Parents	Parochial School Parents	High School Juniors & Seniors
	%	%	%	%	%
Yes	75	74	75	80	76
No	16	14	19	15	23
No opinion	9	12	6	5	1
	100	100	100	100	100

Do you think the students here would get higher scores than students in similar communities, or not so high?

	National Totals	No Children In School	Public School Parents	Parochial School Parents	High School Juniors & Seniors
	%	%	%	%	%
Our students higher	21	18	25	21	26
Our students not so high	15	15	18	14	19
About the same	44	44	40	49	47
Don't know	20	23	17	16	8
	100	100	100	100	100

Should each teacher be paid on the basis of the quality of his work or should all teachers be paid on a standard scale basis?

	National Totals	No Children In School	Public School Parents	Parochial School Parents	High School Juniors & Seniors
	%	%	%	%	%
Quality of work	58	57	61	52	59
Standard scale basis	36	36	35	43	39
No opinion	6	7	4	5	2
	100	100	100	100	100

Would you favor or oppose a system that would hold teachers and administrators more accountable for the progress of students?

	National Totals	No Children In School	Public School Parents	Parochial School Parents	High School Juniors & Seniors
	%	%	%	%	%
Favor	67	66	68	71	65
Oppose	21	21	21	19	29
No opinion	12	13	11	10	6
	100	100	100	100	100

Many states have "tenure" laws, which means that a teacher cannot be fired except by some kind of court procedure. Are you for giving teachers tenure or are you against tenure?

	National Totals	No Children In School	Public School Parents	Parochial School Parents	High School Juniors & Seniors
	%	%	%	%	%
For	35	38	29	28	30
Against	53	48	60	62	61
No opinion	12	14	11	10	9
	100	100	100	100	100

Have teacher organizations gained too much power over their own salaries and working conditions?

	National Totals	No Children In School	Public School Parents	Parochial School Parents	High School Juniors & Seniors
	%	%	%	%	%
Yes	26	27	25	24	17
No	53	49	58	57	72
No opinion	21	24	17	19	11
	100	100	100	100	100

How do you feel about having guidance counselors in the public schools? Do you think they are worth the added cost?

	National Totals	No Children In School	Public School Parents	Parochial School Parents	High School Juniors & Seniors
	%	%	%	%	%
Yes, worth it	73	69	79	79	83
Not, not worth it	16	17	14	12	16
No opinion	11	14	7	9	1
	100	100	100	100	100

Student Power

Should high school students have more say about what goes on within the school on matters such as curriculum? teachers? school rules? student dress?

	National Totals	No Children In School	Public School Parents	Parochial School Parents	High School Juniors & Seniors
	%	%	%	%	%
Curriculum					
Yes	38	36	40	42	83
No	53	53	55	51	15
No opinion	9	11	5	7	2
	100	100	100	100	100

Teachers

Yes	22	22	22	20	53
No	72	70	74	76	43
No opinion	6	8	4	4	4
	100	100	100	100	100

School rules

Yes	36	34	38	39	77
No	58	58	58	58	22
No opinion	6	8	4	3	1
	100	100	100	100	100

Student dress

Yes	37	35	40	32	76
No	57	57	56	64	23
No opinion	6	8	4	4	1
	100	100	100	100	100

Financial Support

Suppose the local public schools said they needed much more money. As you feel at this time, would you vote to raise taxes for this purpose, or would you vote against raising taxes for this purpose?

	National Totals	No Children In School	Public School Parents	Parochial School Parents
	%	%	%	%
For	37	35	43	37
Against	56	57	53	58
Don't know/ no answer	7	8	4	5
	100	100	100	100

Same question, answers by other categories.

	For %	Against %	Don't Know No Answer %
Sex			
Men	38	56	6
Women	37	56	7
Race			
White	38	56	6
Nonwhite	35	58	7

(Continued on next page)

Education

Elementary grades	28	63	9
High school incomplete	33	60	7
High school complete	33	61	6
Technical, trade, or business school	48	48	4
College incomplete	47	48	5
College graduate	61	33	6

Occupation

Business and professional	54	40	6
Clerical and sales	38	58	4
Farm	32	65	3
Skilled labor	34	61	5
Unskilled labor	29	63	8
Non-labor force	32	59	9

Age

21 to 29 years	45	48	7
30 to 49 years	40	56	4
50 years and over	32	60	8

Religion

Protestant	36	57	7
Roman Catholic	36	59	5
Jewish	59	41	--
All others	45	43	12

Region

East	41	54	5
Midwest	34	58	8
South	36	57	7
West	39	55	6

Income

$15,000 and over	49	47	4
$10,000 to $14,999	41	55	4
$ 7,000 to $ 9,999	40	55	5
$ 5,000 to $ 6,999	31	59	10
$ 4,000 to $ 4,999	33	56	11
$ 3,000 to $ 3,999	27	66	7
Under $2,999	27	64	9

Community size

500,000 and over	38	56	6
50,000 to 499,999	36	57	7
25,000 to 49,999	49	49	2
Under 25,000	37	57	6

It has been suggested that state taxes be increased for everyone in order to let the state government pay a greater share of school expense and to reduce local property taxes.

Would you favor an increase in state taxes so that real estate taxes could be lowered on local property?

	National Totals %	No Children In School %	Public School Parents %	Parochial School Parents %
For	54	54	53	61
Against	34	34	36	32
No opinion	12	12	11	7
	100	100	100	100

Tax Aid for Parochial and Private Schools

It has been proposed that some government tax money be used to help parochial schools make ends meet. How do you feel about this? Do you favor or oppose giving some government tax money to help parochial schools?

	National Totals %	No Children In School %	Public School Parents %	Parochial School Parents %	High School Juniors & Seniors %
Favor	48	47	47	59	56
Oppose	44	44	47	33	36
No opinion	8	9	6	8	8
	100	100	100	100	100

In some nations, the government allots a certain amount of money for each child for his education. The parents can then send the child to any public, parochial, or private school they choose. Would you like to see such an idea adopted in this country?

	National Totals %	No Children In School %	Public School Parents %	Parochial School Parents %	High School Juniors & Seniors %
Favor	43	43	41	48	66

(Continued on next page)

Oppose	46	46	48	40	27
No opinion	11	11	11	12	7
	100	100	100	100	100

Sex Education in the Schools

Do you approve or disapprove of schools giving courses in sex education?

	National Totals %	No Children In School %	Public School Parents %	Parochial School Parents %	High School Juniors & Seniors %
Approve	65	61	72	71	89
Disapprove	28	32	22	22	8
No opinion	7	7	6	7	3
	100	100	100	100	100

Would you approve or disapprove if these courses discussed birth control?

	National Totals %	No Children In School %	Public School Parents %	Parochial School Parents %	High School Juniors & Seniors %
Approve	56	52	60	63	82
Disapprove	35	38	32	28	12
No opinion	9	10	8	9	6
	100	100	100	100	100

Some girls get married before they are through high school. If they become pregnant, should they be permitted to attend?

	National Totals %	No Children In School %	Public School Parents %	Parochial School Parents %	High School Juniors & Seniors %
Yes	46	45	49	46	57
No	47	47	46	48	38
No opinion	7	8	5	6	5
	100	100	100	100	100

Change and Innovation

Do you feel that the local public schools are not interested enough in trying new ways and methods or are they *too ready* to try new ideas?

	National Totals %	No Children In School %	Public School Parents %	Parochial School Parents %	High School Juniors & Seniors %
Not interested enough	20	21	20	16	43
Too ready to try new ideas	21	20	21	25	19
Just about right	32	25	42	36	34
Don't know	27	34	17	23	4
	100	100	100	100	100

Do you think the school curriculum in your community needs to be changed to meet today's needs or do you think it already meets today's needs?

	National Totals %	No Children In School %	Public School Parents %	Parochial School Parents %	High School Juniors & Seniors %
Needs to be changed	31	31	33	28	58
Already meets needs	46	36	59	57	41
No opinion	23	33	8	15	1
	100	100	100	100	100

Year-Around Schools

To utilize school buildings to the full extent, would you favor keeping the schools open the year around? Parents could chose which three of the four quarters of the year their children would attend. Do you approve or disapprove of this idea?

	National Totals %	No Children In School %	Public School Parents %	Parochial School Parents %	High School Juniors & Seniors %
Approve	42	44	39	36	40
Disapprove	49	45	56	57	58
No opinion	9	11	5	7	2
	100	100	100	100	100

Attitudes Toward Getting More Information About the Public Schools

Would you like to know more about the public schools in this community?

	National Totals %	No Children In School %	Public School Parents %	Parochial School Parents %	High School Juniors & Seniors %
Yes	54	48	62	54	51
No	44	50	36	41	48
Don't know/ no answer	2	2	2	5	1
	100	100	100	100	100

Same question, answers by other categories.

	For %	Against %	Don't Know/ No Answer %
Sex			
Men	49	49	2
Women	58	40	2
Race			
White	53	45	2
Nonwhite	66	31	3
Education			
Elementary grades	46	50	4
High school incomplete	53	44	3
High school complete	62	38	--
Technical, trade, or business school	54	45	1
College incomplete	58	40	2
College graduate	43	52	5

Occupation

Business and professional	56	42	2
Clerical and sales	55	43	2
Farm	57	41	2
Skilled labor	51	47	2
Unskilled labor	62	36	2
Non-labor force	42	54	4

Age

21 to 29 years	66	31	3
30 to 49 years	61	37	2
50 years and over	41	56	3

Religion

Protestant	53	45	2
Roman Catholic	51	47	2
Jewish	73	25	2
All others	60	37	3

Region

East	56	42	2
Midwest	49	49	2
South	59	37	4
West	48	51	1

Income

$15,000 and over	45	51	4
$10,000 to $14,999	58	41	1
$ 7,000 to $ 9,999	59	40	1
$ 5,000 to $ 6,999	57	43	--
$ 4,000 to $ 4,999	46	52	2
$ 3,000 to $ 3,999	47	47	6
Under $2,999	46	49	5

Community size

500,000 and over	55	43	2
50,000 to 499,999	53	46	1
25,000 to 49,999	56	44	--
Under 25,000	53	44	3

How would you appraise your ability to convey your thoughts in writing? read with speed and comprehension? speak correctly, fluently, effectively? develop new ideas, new solutions?

All Students

	Excellent %	Above Average %	Average %	Below Average %	Poor %
Convey your thoughts in writing	7	28	60	4	1

(Continued on next page)

(Continued from preceding page)

Read with speed and comprehension	5	34	48	12	1
Speak correctly, fluently, effectively	7	28	57	8	--
Develop new ideas, new solutions	8	35	50	7	--

Would you say that your vocabulary is excellent, above average, average, below average, poor?

All students	4	26	62	8	--

Composition of the Sample

Analysis of Respondents

National Adults

No children in schools	56%
Public school parents	36%*
Parochial school parents	13%*

*Totals exceed 44% because some parents have children attending more than one kind of school.

High School Juniors and Seniors

Public school students	93%
Parochial school students	6%
Private school students	1%

	All Adults %	High School Juniors & Seniors %
Sex		
Men	48	49
Women	52	51
	100	100
Race		
White	91	89
Nonwhite	9	11
	100	100

Religion

Protestant	64	54
Roman Catholic	26	31
Jewish	3	3
Others	7	12
	100	100

Age

21 to 29 years	20	
30 to 49 years	38	
50 years and over	42	
	100	
Under 15 years		4
16 years		24
17 years		49
18 years		20
19 years and over		3
		100

Occupation

Business and professional	23	28
Clerical and sales	11	12
Farm	6	9
Skilled labor	19	22
Unskilled labor	20	19
Non-labor force	19	7
Undesignated	2	3
	100	100

Income

$15,000 and over	13	13
$10,000 to $14,999	26	36
$ 7,000 to $ 9,999	19	16
$ 5,000 to $ 6,999	18	20
$ 4,000 to $ 4,999	6	5
$ 3,000 to $ 3,999	6	4
Under $2,999	11	3
Undesignated	1	3
	100	100

Region

East	29	29
Midwest	29	30
South	26	26
West	16	15
	100	100

Community size

500,000 and over	32	29
50,000 to 499,999	23	22

(Continued on next page)

25,000 to 49,999	2	3
Under 25,000	43	46
	100	100

Education

Elementary grades	25	
High school incomplete	16	
High school complete	30	Does not apply
Technical, trade, or business school	5	
College incomplete	12	
College graduate	10	
Undesignated	2	
	100	

Chapter 4
Third Annual Survey
Of the Public's Attitudes
Toward the Public Schools

Purpose of the Study

The survey reported here was sponsored by CFK Ltd. as part of an annual series designed to measure and to record the attitude of American citizens toward their public schools.

Each year new areas are covered, as new problems arise. Some questions are repeated from earlier years to measure trends.

The survey this year dealt at length with the problem of school finances, and particularly with possible economies that might be effected. This proved fortuitous, since the survey itself brings to light the fact that in the minds of the people finance is the biggest problem facing the public schools of the nation.

Research Procedure

The Sample. The sample embraced a total of 1,562 adults. It is described as a modified probability sample of the nation. Interviewing was conducted in every area of the country and in all types of communities. These communities, taken together, represent a true microcosm of the nation.

A separate survey was undertaken to learn the views of young men and women. This sample embraced 229 students who are presently enrolled in either the junior or senior class in high school.

The Interviewing Form. Questions included in the questionnaire were selected after many pretests conducted in the interviewing center maintained by the Gallup organizations in Hopewell, N.J.

Time of Interviewing. The field work for this study was conducted during the period of April 20 through 25, 1971.

Major Problems Confronting The Public Schools in 1971

The major problem facing the public schools in 1970 and in 1969, in the opinion of the American people, was discipline. In 1971, finance — how to pay for the schools — is cited most often as the biggest problem with which the local public schools must deal.

During the year, financial problems have grown with the rise in local property taxes in most areas, the increasing costs of education, and a lagging economy that has placed increased burdens on family pocketbooks.

Next in importance, in terms of number of mentions, is the problem of integration/segregation. It is in second place, as it was in 1970.

Difficulties arising out of school integration — busing and in-school troubles in getting whites and blacks to work together amicably — have been widespread enough to keep this problem in its number two position.

It is worth noting that high school juniors and seniors, and parents with children in the public schools, cite the problem of integration less often than do adults who have no children in school and who draw most of their conclusions from the press and television. This latter group believes integration to be the top problem.

Discipline has dropped from first place in 1970 and 1969 to third place in 1971 as a major problem. Undoubtedly the change in the attitude of students on college campuses during this year finds its parallel in the local schools. Also, as will be pointed out in the section on discipline, there is evidence that discipline has been tightened in the public schools, just as it has been in the colleges and universities.

The lack of school rooms and school facilities is considered to be the fourth major problem.

Drug taking is listed among the top five problems by adults; high school juniors and seniors cite it the most important problem.

The problem of "poor" teachers is cited often enough to place sixth in number of mentions. Lack of interest on the part of parents and pupils, the curriculum, the school administration are all mentioned as problems but not frequently enough to place them among the major concerns.

What's Right with the Public Schools?

When citizens are asked to give their views on the biggest problems facing the public schools, they obviously think of negative factors. To give them a chance to tell what is "right," this question was asked in this year's study:

In your own opinion, in what ways are your local *public* **schools particularly good?**

The response most often given to this question is, "The teachers." The very high respect in which teachers are generally held throughout the nation is evidenced in many ways in this study.

The curriculum (courses offered) comes in for the next highest praise, followed by facilities and extracurricular activities.

Such a question provokes generalized comments; however, the answers do indicate a lack of information about the special merits of any school system.

Cutting School Costs

In the present state of the economy and the tight squeeze on the public's financial resources, the question of where school costs can be cut takes on added importance.

Because of the current interest in finding economies in school budgets, a major part of this year's study of the public's attitudes toward the public schools was devoted to discovering which proposals for reducing costs would meet with public approval and which would be opposed.

The problem of financing the schools can be approached from many points of view. In this study a total of 16 proposals for cost cutting were presented to those included in the survey. Also, questions were added to find out the public's reactions to performance contracts and to the use of management firms to look into school costs.

The proposals for reducing school costs were introduced with these words by the interviewer:

> **Suppose your local school board were "forced" to cut some things from school costs because there is not enough money. I am going to read you a list of many ways that have been suggested for reducing school costs. Will you tell me, in the case of each one, whether your opinion is favorable or unfavorable?**

The 16 proposals have been ranked in descending order on the basis of those which drew the most "unfavorable" responses:

	Unfavorable %	Favorable %	No Opinion %
1. Reduce special services such as speech, reading, and hearing therapy	80	10	10
2. Reduce the number of teachers by increasing class sizes	79	11	10
3. Cut all teachers' salaries by a set percentage	77	12	11
4. Reduce janitorial and maintenance services	72	15	13
5. Cut out kindergarten	69	19	12
6. Cut out after-school activities like bands, clubs, athletics, etc.	68	23	9
7. Keep present textbooks and library books although it may mean using outdated materials	68	20	12
8. Cut out the twelfth grade by covering in three years what is now covered in four	58	29	13

9. Reduce the amount of supplies and materials teachers use in classrooms	58	26	16
10. Reduce the number of subjects offered	57	30	13
11. Charge rent for all textbooks instead of providing them free	56	34	10
12. Make parents responsible for getting children to and from school	51	39	10
13. Reduce the number of counselors on the staff	49	32	19
14. Have the school run on a 12-month basis with three-month vacations for students, one-month vacations for teachers	38	47	15
15. Cancel any subjects that do not have the minimum number of students registered	35	52	13
16. Reduce number of administrative personnel	32	50	18

Readers of this report should be reminded that these suggestions for cost cutting by no means exhaust the list of places where economies could be made. It should be pointed out, also, that the responses do not apply to schools where there is no real need to make economies.

The findings reveal a strong reluctance to take drastic measures, or to alter in an important manner any of the current programs and practices.

As will be pointed out later, this does not mean that the public is unwilling to take a new look at school costs and to examine carefully the relationship between performance and costs.

As will be noted from the preceding table, the suggestion for cost cutting that wins the greatest support is the one that calls for a reduction in the number of administrative personnel. This reaction is undoubtedly a generalized one that springs from the belief that all institutions are subject to Parkinson's Law and acquire unneeded personnel unless halted.

Analysis of the views of the different groups included in

the survey shows that persons who have no children in the public schools tend to look more favorably upon many of the suggested economies than do those with children in the schools. For example, those without children in the schools believe that parents should be made responsible for getting their children to and from school. They would also favor reducing the number of counselors on the staff.

This group, likewise, is much more favorable to putting schools on a 12-month basis, with students having three-month vacations and teachers one month. While the national finding on this suggestion shows more in favor than opposed, parents divide rather evenly: 47% approve, 46% oppose. In the survey conducted in 1970, a somewhat different plan — one that offered the choice of three of four quarters of the year — was voted down by a ratio of 49% to 42%.

It is still to be proved that the 12-month plan represents a real saving. If it does, then pressures will almost certainly mount to utilize school buildings and facilities the year-around.

The major groups included in this study, excepting only the students, favor canceling subjects that do not have the minimum number of students registered.

Performance Contracts

The public wants to be sure that it is getting its money's worth, whether it is a matter of buying shoes or paying taxes for the schools.

In many communities the people are perplexed as to why school costs rise so fast. In some cities they cannot understand why their children at the third- or fourth-grade level cannot read.

In the minds of the people, performance contracts apparently satisfy both of these situations. A fixed amount of money is paid, but only if the child meets a given standard.

To see how the public responds to the idea of performance contracts, this question was included on the interviewing form:

In some public schools, educational companies are

given contracts to put in new methods to teach the children in elementary schools certain basic skills, such as how to read. These are called "performance contracts." If the children don't reach a certain level of achievement, the company doesn't get paid for those children who fail to reach the standard. Would you like to have such contracts made here, in this community, if the overall school costs remain about the same?

The number who favor the idea of performance contracts outnumbers the percentage opposed by the ratio of 49% to 28%, but a very sizable group, 23%, have yet to make up their minds about such a development.

Thus the burden of proof rests upon educators who oppose this idea. Unless cogent arguments can be advanced, unless experience proves that this is not an effective way of reaching educational goals at present cost levels, this movement is likely to gain momentum.

Management Experts

Further evidence that the public is not averse to having competent outsiders look into school costs is to be found in the results from another question bearing upon this matter. The question:

Would you favor or oppose the idea of having your school board hire management experts to look into the costs of local schools to see if the educational goals could be achieved at less cost?

Again, the public votes in favor: 54% like this idea, 31% are opposed, and 15% have no opinion.

Strangely enough, parents of school children support this proposal by higher percentages than do those adults who have no children in the schools.

Accountability

Further evidence that the public wants to be sure that it

is getting its money's worth for the tax dollars spent on public education and that the standards of the public schools are high comes from a third question. This one asked about national tests that permit one community's students to be compared with others of a similar kind. The question asked:

Would you like to see the students in the local schools be given national tests so that their educational achievement could be compared with students in other communities?

The results: 70% favor, 21% oppose, 9% have no opinion. These findings are substantially the same as those found in last year's survey.

Many educators insist that educational achievement is difficult to measure, that communities vary to such an extent that comparisons are meaningless, and that a testing program puts undue pressures on both teachers and students to get high scores. But here again the burden of proof rests with those who oppose. The public wants some proof that their schools are good, that they are getting their money's worth. In the absence of other evidence, they will most certainly accept performance on national tests.

Voting Tax Increases

School bond issues have fared no better in 1971 than they did in 1970. The public is reluctant to vote for additional funds; in fact, a majority of all school bond issues throughout the nation have lost out at the voting booths. The percentage of issues voted upon favorably has changed little during the year; it is still in the low forties.

To gauge voter sentiment towards voting tax increases for the public schools, this question was framed:

Suppose the local *public* schools said they needed much more money. As you feel at this time, would you vote to raise taxes for this purpose, or would you vote against raising taxes for this purpose?

When this same question was asked in the survey

conducted last year, the results showed:

For raising taxes	37%
Against raising taxes	56%
No opinion	7%

When the same question was asked this year throughout the nation, the results were substantially the same:

For raising taxes	40%
Against raising taxes	52%
No opinion	8%

The pattern of those who vote favorably on tax increases for the public schools and those who vote against remains constant.

Those who are most inclined to approve tax increases are the better educated, the younger age groups, business and professional people.

The greatest opposition comes from the poorly educated, persons over 50 years of age, low-income groups, and manual laborers.

Another breakdown of the statistical data reveals the attitudes of those with and without children in the schools. In the 1970 survey, these groups voted as follows:

1970

	For Tax Increases %	Against Tax Increases %	No Opinion %
Public school parents	43	53	4
Parochial/private school parents	37	58	5
No children in schools	35	57	8

In 1971 the vote is as follows:

1971

Public school parents	44	49	7
Parochial/private school parents	37	59	4
No children in schools	37	53	10

The pattern again remains constant. Understandably, parents with children in the public schools are more favorably inclined toward tax increases to support the public schools than those who have no children, or those who have children in parochial or private schools.

The heavy tax burden placed upon local property to support the public schools has brought the demand in many areas that the state government assume a greater share of these costs.

To see whether the public would prefer a shift to higher state taxes in return for lower real estate taxes, this question was asked:

It has been suggested that state taxes be increased for everyone in order to let the state government pay a greater share of school expense and to reduce local property taxes. Would you favor an increase in state taxes so that real estate taxes could be lowered on local property?

More persons favor than disapprove this shift, but the margin has declined during the last year. In 1970 the ratio of those in favor to those against was 54% to 34%; in 1971 the ratio is 46% to 37%.

The Voucher System

Most state governments have had to increase taxes for other purposes. The suggestion that these state taxes be increased still further — even as an offset to real estate taxes — apparently meets with little enthusiasm.

The voucher system for allocating public funds to parochial and private schools has been widely debated during the last year. However, this discussion, as measured by the percentage of persons for and against the voucher system, has not changed attitudes to any great extent. The public was opposed to the voucher plan by a small majority in 1970. The same situation obtains in 1971.

The voucher plan was explained to those interviewed in these words in 1970:

In some nations, the government allots a certain

amount of money for each child for his education. The parents can then send the child to any public, parochial, or private school they choose. Would you like to see such an idea adopted in this country?

In 1971 one sentence was added: *"This is called the voucher system."* This sentence, it was felt, would make it clear to the person being interviewed that we were discussing the voucher system.

The national results show about the same division of opinion:

	Favor %	Oppose %	Don't Know %
1970	43	46	11
1971	38	44	18

It can be seen that the ratio of those opposed to those who favor the voucher system shows little change; the percentage of "undecideds" has gone up markedly.

Moreover, the percentage of parochial and private school parents who favor the plan has also shown a marked increase. The plan is so obviously favorable to this group that its increase in popularity is not unexpected.

Fund Raising in the School

In low-income communities the question arises as to whether school children should be asked to bring money to school to pay for a host of things, apart from school lunches. To save embarrassment for the children of the poor, to increase equality of opportunity, and to minimize dropouts, should not the school itself pay these costs, instead of the child?

Most parents, 59% of those with children in the public schools, say their children must bring money from home to pay for supplies and activities and similar items. In the case of high school juniors and seniors, 76% claim they must bring money to pay for such things as books, insurance, field trips, school pictures, class dues, locker fees, school newspapers and yearbooks, athletic equipment, and the like.

When asked whether the pupil or the school should pay

for such things, the majority say such fees should continue to be paid for by the student, not the school.

The vote is 4 to 1 in favor of continuing the present practice.

Another aspect of this same problem has to do with fund-raising events held by teachers and students to pay for special projects such as after-school activities, school equipment, and the like. There is little opposition to these fund-raising affairs. In fact, the vote in favor is an overwhelming 84%.

The approval vote for this type of fund raising is so high that it leads to the suggestion that the schools of the nation not only should permit, but actively encourage, this method of raising money for school activities. Yet professional educators find many drawbacks to certain fund-raising activities of this sort, often with good logic.

Parent Accountability

Much discussion in educational circles has centered about teacher and school accountability. In the survey this year, for the first time, the matter of *parent* accountability was explored — with results so significant that a change in focus of the present debate is indicated.

The question that was designed to gather the views of the public on this matter of parent accountability, as opposed to teacher, school, and pupil accountability, was stated as follows:

When some children do poorly in school, some people place the blame on the children, some on the children's home life, some on the school, and some on the teachers. Of course, all of these things share the blame, but where would you place the *chief* blame?

The answer given by the greatest percentage of those interviewed: the children's home life. In fact, more than half of the adults interviewed (54%) give this answer. Only 14% name children, 8% teachers, and 6% the schools.

It is significant that parents with children now in the public schools name the child's home life as the chief cause of a student's failure in school; they do not, as might be expected, shift the responsibility to the teachers or to the school or to the children.

It is equally interesting that high school juniors and seniors do not absolve themselves from blame for doing poorly. When the same question was put to them, they said the student, himself, is to blame. Approximately one-half (51%) blame the children, 25% say "home life," only 11% blame the teachers, and only 5% the school.

To explore further the matter of parental accountability, the following question was included:

A suggestion has been made that parents of school children attend one evening class a month to find out what they can do at home to improve their children's behavior and increase their interest in school work. Is it a good idea or a poor idea?

Eight in 10 (81%) of all adults questioned thought this was a good idea. Most important, virtually this same ratio (80%) of the parents of school children said it was a good idea.

This very impressive percentage reveals a growing recognition of the role of parents in the educational process, and of the need for a new kind of partnership between teachers and parents.

Since an important part of the whole educational process must necessarily be carried on in the home, it is obvious that parents must be better trained to carry out their responsibilities.

Until this point in history, the schools have had to shoulder the burden — teaching discipline and how to get along with others, developing proper work habits, providing motivation, and doing a dozen other things — all in addition to teaching the basic school subjects and skills.

Other surveys have shown how important home training and motivation are in determining a child's success in school — in fact, in determining how far he is likely to go in his education.

Preparing parents to carry out their educational responsibilities is just as important as training teachers for their work. How best to do this must await the results of experiments planned in this new field of educational training.

What is of utmost importance is that parents themselves see the need for this kind of training. They are willing to devote time to learn how to do a better job of motivating their children, improving their behavior, and covering those areas of education not included in the school curriculum.

Discipline

Because of the great concern on the part of the public about discipline in the public schools, an effort was made in the 1971 survey to probe more deeply into this problem with the hope of shedding more light on the views of parents and other groups.

This year, as last, those interviewed express their belief that discipline is "not strict enough." There has been a slight decrease in the number who hold this opinion during the last year, and, as pointed out earlier, the problem of discipline has been superseded by finance as the number one worry about the public schools; yet there has been only a slight change in views recorded.

Here is a comparison of the findings for the two years — 1970 and 1971.

	1970 %	1971 %
Discipline is too strict	2	3
Discipline is not strict enough	53	48
Discipline is about right	31	33
Don't know/no opinion	14	16

The matter of discipline has not commanded the front-page space it did a year ago, nor as much television or radio time. Some evidence that the schools may be imposing stricter discipline comes from the interviews with high school juniors and seniors — who would be immediately concerned.

When they were asked a year ago whether they thought discipline was "too strict" or "not strict enough," 15% said it was "too strict," 23% said it was "not strict enough," and the remainder said it was "about right." This year almost exactly the same number say discipline is "too strict" as say it is "not strict enough" — 22% to 23%.

Since discipline means different things to different people, a question was asked this year of those who replied that discipline is "not strict enough." If they gave this response they were then asked:

Can you tell me what you mean? In what way is discipline not strict enough?

Those who said that discipline was not strict enough gave answers that have been categorized as follows:

Teachers lack authority to keep order	11%
Students have too much freedom; they can get away with anything	11%
Students have no respect for their teachers; pay no attention to them	6%
Rules are not enforced	3%
Vandalism	2%
Other responses and no opinion	11%

The problem of discipline has two sides. One concerns the enforcement of rules; the other, avoiding the need to enforce rules.

The public, judging from their responses, is strongly of the opinion that "if the schools and the teachers interest the children in learning, most disciplinary problems disappear."

Every group interviewed, and by substantial majorities, agrees that the need for discipline tends to disappear when students become genuinely interested in learning.

Further evidence on this point comes from the findings on another question included in the survey. This one dealt with problem children and what should be done about them. The question was worded in this fashion:

Some students are not interested in school. Often they keep other students from working in school. What should be done in these cases?

Answers fall into two broad categories: "use punitive measures" (expel them, use harsher discipline, put them into a school for problem students) and "try remedial measures" (special classes, a more interesting curriculum, vocational training, etc.).

Those who fall into this latter category outnumber those who believe in punitive measures by a 2-to-1 ratio.

Racial Integration in the Schools

The 1954 Supreme Court decision dealing with racial integration in the schools was based largely upon the assumption that black students, segregated in their own schools, were being deprived of the higher quality of education offered whites. Some 17 years have passed since that time and integration* is far from complete.

In fact, problems arising out of school integration are cited, in this survey, as the nation's greatest public school problem, next to finance.

Some individuals doubt that integrated education is actually improving the quality of education received by the blacks, or whether it is improving the quality of education received by the whites; and whether integration actually is improving relations between the races.

To see how the public would respond to questions dealing with these aspects of school integration, the following questions were included in the present survey:

1. Do you feel it (school integration) has improved the quality of education received by black students?
2. Do you feel it (school integration) has improved the quality of education received by white students?
3. Do you feel it (school integration) has improved relations between blacks and whites or has it worked against better relations?

The national consensus, judged by survey results, is that integration has improved the quality of education received by the blacks, that is has not improved the quality of education received by white students, but that, on the

*Not distinguished in this report from desegregation.

whole, it has improved relations between blacks and whites.

Parents of children now enrolled in the public schools say, by a ratio of 44% to 35%, that relations have been improved; parents of children in parochial and private schools, by a ratio of 49% to 39%, believe that relations have improved. And perhaps of greatest significance, high school juniors and seniors are even more of the opinion that integration has improved relations. They hold 59% to 28% that relations have improved.

Educational Innovation

The American people are almost evenly divided on the question of whether too many or not enough educational changes are being tried in the public schools.

The question asked in the survey taps generalized attitudes and, as will be pointed out later, does not apply to specific innovations contemplated. These must be considered on their own merits.

What the question does probe is the overall feeling of the public about the extent to which the schools are keeping up with the times.

In the survey of last year, this question was asked:

Do you feel that the local public schools are not interested enough in trying new ways and methods, or are they too ready to try new ideas?

The same attitude was probed this year from a slightly different direction, one dealing more with behavior. The question this year reads:

In the schools in your community, do you think too many educational changes are being tried, or not enough?

No matter which way attitudes are measured, the answers come back almost exactly the same, as the following findings reveal.

1970		1971	
Do you feel that the local public schools are not interested enough in trying new ways and methods or are they too ready to try new ideas?		In the schools in your community, do you think too many educational changes are being tried, or not enough?	
Not interested enough	20%	Too many being tried	22%
Too ready to try new ideas	21%	Not enough	24%
Just about right	32%	Just about right	32%
Don't know	27%	Don't know	22%

Students do not agree with their elders on this matter. In both surveys, they vote heavily on the side that not enough innovations are being tried, that not enough interest is being displayed in trying new methods. In fact, they hold this belief by a ratio of 3 to 1.

As noted earlier, the reaction of those interviewed was to the generalized issue of change, not to specific innovations proposed.

For example:

By a very large majority all the major groups surveyed hold the opinion that not enough attention is being given to students who do not plan to go on to college.

Nationally, the findings show that 68% agree with those who believe "that too much emphasis is placed in the high schools on preparing students for college and not enough emphasis on preparing students for occupations that do not require a college degree." In contrast to the 68% who hold this view, only 23% hold the opposite view.

Another case in point concerns the amount of time spent in classrooms as opposed to the time spent in independent study. A plurality of the adults included in the survey believe the local schools should give more time for independent study, the ratio being 31% in favor to 22% opposed.

The junior and senior high school students questioned are strongly of the opinion that more time should be spent in independent study, relatively less in the classroom. Their vote is 56% in favor to 18% opposed.

The Major Problems

What do you think are the biggest problems with which the *public* schools in this community must deal?

	National Totals %	No Children In Schools %	Public School Parents %	Parochial School Parents %	High School Juniors & Seniors %
Finances	23	22	24	21	9
Integration/ segregation	21	26	16	14	17
Discipline	14	13	14	23	14
Facilities	13	10	17	20	18
Dope/drugs	12	11	13	9	19
Teachers' lack of interest/ ability	5	4	5	12	7
Teachers (general)	6	4	8	5	5
Parents' lack of interest	4	3	5	5	*
School adminis- tration	3	3	3	7	3
Curriculum	3	3	2	5	5
Pupils' lack of interest	2	2	2	--	3
Vandalism	2	2	2	*	6
Disrespect for teachers	2	2	1	*	1
School board policies	1	*	2	*	1
Using new up-to-date methods	1	*	2	*	*
We have no problems	4	3	6	*	3
Miscellaneous	6	6	5	9	14
Don't know/ no answer	12	16	8	10	2

*Less than 1%

In your own opinion, in what ways are your local *public* schools particularly good?

	National Totals %	No Children In Schools %	Public School Parents %	Parochial School Parents %	High School Juniors & Seniors %
Teachers	21	17	27	22	27

(Continued on next page)

Curriculum	15	10	22	18	28
Facilities	9	6	13	13	10
Up-to-date teaching methods	5	4	7	3	1
Extracurricular activities	3	2	5	5	14
No racial conflicts	3	3	4	3	3
Small school/ classes	2	2	3	2	3
Good administration	2	2	3	3	*
Good student-teacher relationships	2	1	3	*	4
Parents are interested/ participate	2	*	3	4	--
Discipline	1	1	1	*	2
Transportation system	1	*	2	--	*
Equal opportunity for all	1	1	1	4	*
Nothing good	7	7	7	13	8
Miscellaneous	4	4	8	2	10
Don't know/ no answer	27	38	12	23	10

*Less than 1%

Cutting School Costs

Suppose your local school board were "forced" to cut some things from school costs because there is not enough money. I am going to read you a list of many ways that have been suggested for reducing school costs. Will you tell me, in the case of each one, whether your opinion is favorable or unfavorable.

	National Totals %	No Children In Schools %	Public School Parents %	Parochial School Parents %	High School Juniors & Seniors %

Reduce the number of teachers by increasing class sizes.

Favorable	11	12	9	14	8
Unfavorable	79	72	88	86	91
No opinion	10	16	3	--	1
	100	100	100	100	100

Cut all teachers' salaries by a set percentage.

Favorable	12	13	11	14	15
Unfavorable	77	70	85	84	80
No opinion	11	17	4	2	5
	100	100	100	100	100

Cut out after-school activities like bands, clubs, athletics, etc.

Favorable	23	22	23	31	8
Unfavorable	68	64	74	68	89
No opinion	9	14	3	1	3
	100	100	100	100	100

Have the schools run on a 12-month basis with three-month vacations for students, one month for teachers.

Favorable	47	45	47	57	37
Unfavorable	38	33	46	34	58
No opinion	15	22	7	9	5
	100	100	100	100	100

Make parents responsible for getting children to and from school.

Favorable	39	41	36	48	27
Unfavorable	51	43	62	51	68
No opinion	10	16	2	1	5
	100	100	100	100	100

Cut out kindergarten.

Favorable	19	18	21	23	24
Unfavorable	69	64	75	72	71
No opinion	12	18	4	5	5
	100	100	100	100	100

Charge rent for all textbooks instead of providing them free.

Favorable	34	33	33	47	33
Unfavorable	56	52	63	51	65
No opinion	10	15	4	2	2
	100	100	100	100	100

Cut out the twelfth grade by covering in three years what is now covered in four.

Favorable	29	31	26	28	45
Unfavorable	58	51	69	65	53
No opinion	13	18	5	7	2
	100	100	100	100	100

Cancel any subjects that do not have the minimum number of students registered.

Favorable	52	51	52	60	53
Unfavorable	35	31	42	35	45
No opinion	13	18	6	5	2
	100	100	100	100	100

Reduce the number of subjects offered.

Favorable	30	30	29	32	17
Unfavorable	57	50	68	65	82
No opinion	13	20	3	3	1
	100	100	100	100	100

Reduce janitorial and maintenance services.

Favorable	15	15	14	16	19
Unfavorable	72	67	80	78	77
No opinion	13	18	6	6	4
	100	100	100	100	100

Keep present textbooks and library books although it may mean using outdated materials.

Favorable	20	20	20	14	16
Unfavorable	68	63	76	82	81
No opinion	12	17	4	4	3
	100	100	100	100	100

Reduce the amount of supplies and materials teachers use in classrooms.

Favorable	26	27	22	31	26
Unfavorable	58	51	70	60	73
No opinion	16	22	8	9	1
	100	100	100	100	100

Reduce the number of counselors on the staff.

Favorable	32	31	33	40	28
Unfavorable	49	42	58	49	70
No opinion	19	27	9	11	2
	100	100	100	100	100

Reduce special services, such as speech, reading, and hearing therapy.

Favorable	10	10	9	9	13
Unfavorable	80	74	89	89	84
No opinion	10	16	2	2	3
	100	100	100	100	100

Reduce the number of administrative personnel.

Favorable	50	48	50	55	43
Unfavorable	32	27	41	32	52
No opinion	18	25	9	13	5
	100	100	100	100	100

In some public schools, educational companies are given contracts to put in new methods to teach the children in elementary schools certain basic skills, such as how to read. These are called "performance contracts." If the children don't reach a certain level of achievement, the company doesn't get paid for those children who fail to reach the standard. Would you like to have such contracts made here, in this community, if the overall school costs remain about the same?

	National Totals %	No Children In Schools %	Public School Parents %	Parochial School Parents %	High School Juniors & Seniors %
Yes	49	44	55	58	57
No	28	25	33	24	33
No opinion	23	31	12	18	10
	100	100	100	100	100

Would you favor or oppose the idea of having your school board hire management experts to look into the costs of local schools to see if the educational goals could be achieved at less cost?

	National Totals %	No Children In Schools %	Public School Parents %	Parochial School Parents %	High School Juniors & Seniors %
Favor	54	49	61	67	69
Oppose	31	30	33	24	23
Don't know	15	21	6	9	8
	100	100	100	100	100

Would you like to see the students in the local schools be given national tests so that their educational achievement could be compared with students in other communities?

	National Totals %	No Children In Schools %	Public School Parents %	Parochial School Parents %	High School Juniors & Seniors %
Yes	70	69	72	70	66
No	21	20	22	24	31
No opinion	9	11	6	6	3
	100	100	100	100	100

The Voucher System

In some nations, the government allots a certain amount of money for each child for his education. The parents can then send the child to any public, parochial, or private school they choose. This is called the "voucher system." Would you like to see such an idea adopted in this country?

	National Totals %	No Children In Schools %	Public School Parents %	Parochial School Parents %	High School Juniors & Seniors %
Favor	38	34	39	66	58
Oppose	44	40	51	31	35
No opinion	18	26	10	3	7
	100	100	100	100	100

Voting Tax Increases

Suppose the local *public* schools said they needed much more money. As you feel at this time, would you vote to raise taxes for this purpose, or would you vote against raising taxes for this purpose?

	National Totals %	No Children In Schools %	Public School Parents %	Parochial School Parents %	High School Juniors & Seniors %
For	40	37	44	37	45

Against	52	53	49	59	49
No opinion	8	10	7	4	6
	100	100	100	100	100

Same question, answers by different categories.

	For %	Against %	Don't Know/ No Answer %
Sex			
Men	40	53	7
Women	39	52	9
Race			
White	40	53	7
Nonwhite	38	49	13
Education			
Elementary grades	27	62	11
High school incomplete	32	60	8
High school complete	37	55	8
Technical, trade, or business school	42	49	9
College incomplete	48	46	6
College graduate	58	35	7
Occupation			
Business and professional	52	41	7
Clerical and sales	48	48	4
Farm	34	56	10
Skilled labor	38	54	8
Unskilled labor	35	59	6
Non-labor force	27	60	13
Age			
21 to 29 years	53	40	7
30 to 49 years	43	52	5
50 years and over	31	58	11
Religion			
Protestant	41	51	8
Roman Catholic	34	57	9
Jewish	50	39	11
All others	42	47	11
Region			
East	34	58	8
Midwest	40	52	8
South	41	50	9
West	46	46	8
Community size			
500,000 and over	39	51	10
50,000 to 499,999	38	52	10

(Continued on next page)

25,000 to 49,999	57	36	7
Under 25,000	40	55	5
Income			
$15,000 and over	51	42	7
$10,000 to $14,999	41	51	8
$ 7,000 to $ 9,999	42	55	3
$ 5,000 to $ 6,999	38	52	10
$ 3,000 to $ 4,999	36	55	9
Under $3,000	24	60	16

It has been suggested that state taxes be increased for everyone in order to let the state government pay a greater share of school expense and to reduce local property taxes. Would you favor an increase in state taxes so that real estate taxes could be lowered on local property?

	National Totals %	No Children In Schools %	Public School Parents %	Parochial School Parents %	High School Juniors & Seniors %
For	46	43	50	46	50
Against	37	36	38	46	31
No opinion	17	21	12	8	19
	100	100	100	100	100

Fund Raising in the Public Schools

Does your child bring money from home to pay for anything, except lunch, in school? [Asked only of parents of school children]

	National Totals %	Public School Parents %	Parochial School Parents %	High School Juniors & Seniors %
Yes	59	60	56	76
No	39	38	37	24
Don't know	2	2	7	--
	100	100	100	100

If *"yes,"* for what?

Books	9	19	27	30

Supplies for classes (general)	7	17	17	24
Travel expenses for field trips	5	11	11	7
Athletic fees/equipment	3	6	6	11
School newspaper/school-related newspaper	3	7	2	7
Fees for special programs	3	8	5	4
Club dues/class dues	2	5	3	16
Parties/dances	2	4	3	2
Charitable contributions/events	2	3	6	3
General school activities	1	3	4	5
Miscellaneous	9	20	12	26

Do you think such fees should be charged?

	National Totals %	Public School Parents %	Parochial School Parents %	High School Juniors & Seniors %
Yes	47	47	46	56
No	10	11	10	17
No opinion	2	2	--	3
	59	60	56	76

In some schools, teachers and students have fund-raising events to finance special projects for school equipment, after-school activities, and the like. Do you think it is a good idea or a poor idea for the schools to permit these events?

	National Totals %	No Children In Schools %	Public School Parents %	Parochial School Parents %	High School Juniors & Seniors %
Good idea	84	81	88	90	97
Poor idea	11	12	10	8	3
No opinion	5	7	2	2	--
	100	100	100	100	100

Parent Accountability

When some children do poorly in school, some people place the blame on the children, some on the children's home life, some on the school, and some on the teachers. Of course, all of these things share the blame, but where would you place the *chief* blame?

	National Totals %	No Children In Schools %	Public School Parents %	Parochial School Parents %	High School Juniors & Seniors %
Children	14	11	17	14	51
Home life	54	58	49	44	25
School	6	6	6	14	5
Teachers	8	7	10	8	11
No opinion	18	18	18	20	8
	100	100	100	100	100

A suggestion has been made that parents of school children attend one evening class a month to find out what they can do at home to improve their children's behavior and increase their interest in school work. Is it a good idea or a poor idea?

	National Totals %	No Children In Schools %	Public School Parents %	Parochial School Parents %	High School Juniors & Seniors %
Good idea	81	82	80	81	75
Poor idea	13	11	16	15	21
No opinion	6	7	4	4	4
	100	100	100	100	100

Discipline

How do you feel about the discipline in the local public schools — is it too strict, not strict enough, or just about right?

	National Totals %	No Children In Schools %	Public School Parents %	Parochial School Parents %	High School Juniors & Seniors %
Too strict	3	3	3	--	22
Not strict enough	48	47	47	58	23
Just about right	33	26	46	29	53

	National Totals %	No Children In Schools %	Public School Parents %	Parochial School Parents %	High School Juniors & Seniors %
Don't know	16	24	4	13	2
	100	100	100	100	100

If "not strict enough": Can you tell me what you mean? In what ways is discipline not strict enough?

	National Totals %	No Children In Schools %	Public School Parents %	Parochial School Parents %	High School Juniors & Seniors %
Teachers lack authority	11	10	12	14	2
Students have too much freedom	11	11	12	15	7
Disrespect for teachers	6	7	4	8	4
Rules are not enforced	3	4	2	3	4
Dress code is too liberal	3	2	3	4	*
Vandalism	2	2	2	5	*
Parents not interested in school affairs	2	1	3	5	*
Miscellaneous	3	3	3	5	*
Don't know/ no answer	3	3	4	2	*

*Less than 1%

Some students are not interested in school. Often they keep other students from working in school. What should be done in these cases?

	National Totals %	No Children In Schools %	Public School Parents %	Parochial School Parents %	High School Juniors & Seniors %
Special classes for all who are not interested	29	26	34	27	27
Expel them	12	12	12	13	22
Offer better/ more interesting: curriculum/teaching methods	11	11	10	13	14

(Continued on next page)

Special coun- seling	9	9	10	11	13
Harsher discipline	9	9	10	7	4
Vocational training	8	8	7	9	8
Make their parents responsible	7	6	7	8	3
Put in school for problem students	6	5	7	13	3
Teachers should take more in- terest in such students	4	3	5	3	4
Miscellaneous	5	5	5	4	5
Don't know/ no answer	18	21	16	14	14

Some people say that if the schools and the teachers interest the children in learning, most disciplinary problems disappear. Do you agree or disagree?

	National Totals %	No Children In Schools %	Public School Parents %	Parochial School Parents %	High School Juniors & Seniors %
Agree	76	75	76	78	81
Disagree	18	17	20	20	18
No opinion	6	8	4	2	1
	100	100	100	100	100

Racial Integration in the Schools

How do you feel about school integration?

Do you feel it has improved the quality of education received by black students?

	National Totals %	No Children In Schools %	Public School Parents %	Parochial School Parents %	High School Juniors & Seniors %
Yes	43	39	48	51	56
No	31	31	31	33	31

Don't know	26	30	21	16	13
	100	100	100	100	100

Do you feel it has improved the quality of education received by white students?

	National Totals %	No Children In Schools %	Public School Parents %	Parochial School Parents %	High School Juniors & Seniors %
Yes	23	21	26	30	35
No	51	48	54	53	47
Don't know	26	31	20	17	18
	100	100	100	100	100

Do you feel it has improved relations between blacks and whites or has it worked against better relations?

	National Totals %	No Children In Schools %	Public School Parents %	Parochial School Parents %	High School Juniors & Seniors %
Improved relations	40	36	44	49	59
Worked against	35	35	35	39	28
No opinion	25	29	21	12	13
	100	100	100	100	100

Same question, answers by different categories.

	Improved Relations %	Worked Against %	No Opinion %
Sex			
Men	40	37	23
Women	40	33	27
Race			
White	37	37	26
Nonwhite	63	15	22
Education			
Elementary grades	26	43	31
High school incomplete	36	37	27
High school complete	37	38	25
Technical, trade, or business school	41	34	25

(Continued on next page)

College incomplete	49	32	19
College graduate	51	29	20

Occupation

Business and professional	49	28	23
Clerical and sales	44	31	25
Farm	29	37	34
Skilled labor	40	39	21
Unskilled labor	40	34	26
Non-labor force	29	40	31

Age

21 to 29 years	50	31	19
30 to 49 years	42	36	22
50 years and over	33	36	31

Religion

Protestant	39	37	24
Roman Catholic	39	33	28
Jewish	48	35	17
All others	48	22	30

Region

East	37	34	29
Midwest	40	36	24
South	41	39	20
West	42	29	29

Income

$15,000 and over	44	35	21
$10,000 to $14,999	41	35	24
$ 7,000 to $ 9,999	40	37	23
$ 5,000 to $ 6,999	42	33	25
$ 3,000 to $ 4,999	38	37	25
Under $3,000	31	35	34

Community size

500,000 and over	41	37	22
50,000 to 499,999	43	33	24
25,000 to 49,999	32	61	7
Under 25,000	37	34	29

Educational Innovation

In the schools in your community, do you think too many educational changes are being tried, or not enough?

	National Totals %	No Children In Schools %	Public School Parents %	Parochial School Parents %	High School Juniors & Seniors %
Too many	22	21	23	24	14
Not enough	24	23	26	33	53
About right	32	24	44	28	31
Don't know	22	32	7	15	2
	100	100	100	100	100

In some schools, time spent by students in classrooms is being reduced to give more time for independent study, that is, carrying out learning projects on their own. Should the local schools give more time to independent study than they presently do, or should they give less time?

	National Totals %	No Children In Schools %	Public School Parents %	Parochial School Parents %	High School Juniors & Seniors %
More	31	30	31	39	56
Less	22	18	26	28	18
About right now	25	21	32	25	20
No opinion	22	31	11	8	6
	100	100	100	100	100

Some people feel that too much emphasis is placed in the high schools on preparing students for college and not enough emphasis on preparing students for occupations that do not require a college degree. Do you agree or disagree?

	National Totals %	No Children In Schools %	Public School Parents %	Parochial School Parents %	High School Juniors & Seniors %
Agree	68	68	69	67	61
Disagree	23	21	25	27	35
No opinion	9	11	6	6	4
	100	100	100	100	100

Analysis of Respondents

Adults

No children in school	56%
Public school parents	39%*
Parochial school parents	8%*

*Totals exceed 44% because some parents have children attending more than one kind of school.

High school juniors and seniors

Public school students	90%
Parochial and private school students	10%

	All Adults %	High School Juniors & Seniors %
Sex		
Men	48	52
Women	52	48
	100	100
Race		
White	91	90
Nonwhite	9	10
	100	100
Religion		
Protestant	64	53
Roman Catholic	26	33
Jewish	3	4
Others	7	10
	100	100
Age		
21 to 29 years	20	
30 to 49 years	38	
50 years and over	42	
	100	
15 years and under		10
16 years		30
17 years		42
18 years and over		18
		100
Region		
East	29	31
Midwest	28	30

South	26	25
West	17	14
	100	100

Community size

500,000 and over	32	32
50,000 to 499,999	24	23
25,000 to 49,999	3	3
Under 25,000	41	42
	100	100

Education

Elementary grades	16	
High school incomplete	19	
High school complete	31	Does not apply
Technical, trade, or business school	7	
College incomplete	13	
College graduate	14	
	100	

Occupation

Business and professional	24	29
Clerical and sales	11	13
Farm	5	6
Skilled labor	18	23
Unskilled labor	21	21
Non-labor force	19	4
Undesignated	2	4
	100	100

Income

$15,000 and over	17	18
$10,000 to $14,999	26	32
$ 7,000 to $ 9,999	18	14
$ 5,000 to $ 6,999	15	15
$ 4,000 to $ 4,999	5	4
$ 3,000 to $ 3,999	5	5
Under $2,999	12	4
Undesignated	2	8
	100	100

Chapter 5
Fourth Annual Gallup Poll of Public Attitudes Toward Education

Purpose of the Study

The survey reported in the following pages was sponsored by CFK Ltd. and is the fourth in an annual series designed to measure and record the attitude of American citizens toward their public schools.

Each year new areas are covered as new problems become salient. Some questions are repeated from earlier years in order to measure trends.

The survey this year emphasized various ways of providing funds for the operation of public schools in the United States. Other issues which provoke discussion in the educational world were included: the goals of education, accountability, compulsory attendance, teacher tenure, alternative ways for students to learn, the public's attitudes towards school boards and teachers.

The findings of this study apply to the nation as a whole and not necessarily to any single community. These findings do, however, permit local communities to compare results of surveys conducted within their own community with the results of the national survey.

The study represents the joint planning of the staff of CFK Ltd. and the staff of Gallup International. Valuable help in selection of the areas of interest and concern to be included in the survey came from: Forbes Bottomly, superintendent of schools, Seattle, Wash.; B. Frank Brown, director, Information and Services Division, Institute for

Development of Educational Activities (I/D/E/A), Melbourne, Fla., and member, CFK Ltd. Board of Directors; Stanley Elam, editor, *Phi Delta Kappan,* Bloomington, Ind.; Ernest Jones, acting superintendent of schools, St. Louis, Mo.; Carl L. Marburger, state commissioner of education, Trenton, N.J.; and Kenneth Schoonover, superintendent, Arapahoe County School District Six, Littleton, Colo.

Research Procedure

The Sample. The sample embraced a total of 1,614 adults. It is described as a modified probability sample of the nation. Interviewing was conducted in every area of the country and in all types of communities. These communities, taken together, represent a true microcosm of the nation. A full description of the adult sample will be found at the end of this report.

A separate survey was undertaken to learn the views of professional educators. This sample embraced 270 educators (teachers, assistant principals, principals, administrators, superintendents). These persons also were interviewed in every area of the country and in all types of communities.

The Interviewing Form. Questions included in the questionnaire were selected after many pretests conducted in the interviewing center maintained by the Gallup organizations in Hopewell, New Jersey.

Time of Interviewing. The field work for this study was done from April 21 through 23, 1972.

Major Problems Confronting
The Public Schools in 1972

Discipline again ranks as the number one problem of the public schools, in the minds of the citizens of the nation. For one brief year, 1971, it dropped to third place in the list. This year discipline is restored to the top position held in earlier years.

Based upon the number of mentions to the open question, "What do you think are the biggest problems with

which the *public* schools in this community must deal?,"
the top problems are as follows:

1. Lack of discipline
2. Lack of proper financial support
3. Integration-segregation problems
4. Difficulty of getting "good" teachers
5. Large school, too large classes
6. Parents' lack of interest
7. Lack of proper facilities
8. Poor curriculum
9. Use of dope, drugs

Since last year the number of times the use of dope and drugs was mentioned as a serious problem of the schools has dropped significantly — from fifth place in 1971 to ninth place in 1972.

The professional educators interviewed in this same survey regard school finances as the number one problem, followed in order by integration/segregation, discipline, parents' lack of interest, quality of teaching, curriculum, use of dope and drugs, and lack of proper school facilities.

The public's desire for stricter school policies bearing on discipline has been manifested in many ways in the years since these annual CFK Ltd. surveys were established. The present survey adds further evidence.

The question of "student rights" was probed in the present survey. The question:

Generally speaking, do the local public school students in this community have too many rights and privileges, or not enough?

The general public replied:

Too many	41%
Not enough	11%
Just right	33%
No opinion	15%

Since 18-year-olds now have the right to vote, the question has arisen as to whether, as full-fledged citizens, they should not have more rights than other students. The public says "no" in resounding fashion. The question:

Should students who are 18 years of age, and now have the right to vote, have more rights and privileges than other students?

Yes	21%
No	73%
No opinion	6%

It is worth noting again that in the 1971 survey the public agreed, by a substantial majority, that while discipline is a major concern, "if the schools and teachers interest the children in learning, most disciplinary problems disappear."

In What Ways Are the Local Public Schools Particularly Good?

Relatively few citizens ever stop to think about the good things the public schools are doing. It is much easier to complain. To find out just what the typical citizen thinks his own schools are "doing right," this question has been included in all CFK Ltd. surveys:

In your own opinion, in what ways are your local *public* schools particularly good?

The responses, in order of mention, follow:

1. The curriculum
2. The teachers
3. School facilities
4. Equal opportunity for all
5. No racial conflicts
6. Extracurricular activities
7. Up-to-date teaching methods
8. Good student-teacher relationships
9. Good administration
10. Small school or small classes

Because of the absence of objective data by which to judge local schools, responses are almost never stated in terms of achievement, of success in reaching educational goals, or the product itself — the graduates.

Even professional educators are unlikely to judge the schools by results. When they were asked this same question, they named, in order: curriculum, teachers, equal opportunity for all students, school facilities, up-to-date teaching methods, no racial conflicts, good student-teacher relationships, extracurricular activities, good administration, small school or small classes.

The Goals of Education
As the Public Sees Them

Most efforts to discover the public's ideas on the goals of education have ended in questionable findings because researchers have failed to distinguish between ends and means.

To avoid this, the present survey has attempted to make a separation, dealing with ends first and with means later.

An open question (with two probes) was utilized to get at the public's ideas of the ultimate goals of education. This was the question asked:

People have different reasons why they want their children to get an education. What are the chief reasons that come to your mind?

After the person interviewed had answered this question, he was asked if he could think of anything else. One further attempt was made to see if he could add to his list.

Here are the responses and the percentages of respondents mentioning each in some form:

1. To get better jobs	44%
2. To get along better with people at all levels of society	43%
3. To make more money — achieve financial success	38%
4. To attain self-satisfaction	21%
5. To stimulate their minds	15%
6. Miscellaneous reasons	11%

These responses show that the public thinks of education largely in a pragmatic way. But this heavy emphasis on material goals, at the expense of those concerned with intellectual and artistic development, should come as no shock. Americans are a practical people who believe firmly that education is the royal road to success in life.

Is there a wide chasm between the educational programs followed in the public schools and the programs to which the public attaches great importance? Some will view these tabulations as evidence that there is. Yet we have already seen that the public does not regard curricular problems as particularly serious. In fact curriculum ranked at the top in our tabulation of school strengths.

After having sought to learn the public's views on the ultimate goals of education, our interviewers handed each respondent a card on which were listed nine specific programs for reaching educational goals.

Respondents were asked first about elementary school children.

Below are ratings of these programs based upon the number of mentions. The question was:

Which three of these educational programs [card list] would you like your local elementary schools (grades 1-6) to give *more attention* **to:**

1. Teaching students the skills of reading, writing, and arithmetic
2. Teaching students how to solve problems and think for themselves
3. Teaching students to respect law and authority
4. Teaching students how to get along with others
5. Teaching students the skills of speaking and listening
6. Teaching students vocational skills
7. Teaching students health and physical education
8. Teaching students about the world of today and yesterday (that is, history, geography, and civics)
9. Teaching students how to compete with others

Respondents were then asked the same question in relation to junior and senior high schools (grades 7-12). In order of mentions:

1. Teaching students to respect law and authority

2. Teaching students how to solve problems and think for themselves

3. Teaching students vocational skills

4. Teaching students how to get along with others

5. Teaching students the skills of speaking and listening

6. Teaching students about the world of today and yesterday (that is, history, geography, and civics)

7. Teaching students the skills of reading, writing, and arithmetic

8. Teaching students health and physical education

9. Teaching students how to compete with others

Voting Financial Help for Schools

School bond issues are still having their difficulties. Throughout the nation more are voted down than are approved.

To shed light on the attitude of voters toward the financial needs and problems of the public schools, this question has been asked in each national survey beginning with 1969:

Suppose the local *public* schools said they needed much more money. As you feel at this time, would you vote to raise taxes for this purpose, or would you vote against raising taxes for this purpose?

The national results again show a greater number voting against rather than for.

For raising taxes	36%
Against raising taxes	56%
No opinion	8%

The pattern of those favoring tax increases and those opposed remains constant from year to year. Those most in favor come from these groups: the better educated, the younger age levels, business and professional people, and white-collar workers.

The most opposition to voting tax increases comes from these groups: the poorly educated, persons over 50 years of age, low income groups, and manual workers.

Interestingly enough, the persons who have suffered most from not having had a good education are the ones most opposed to meeting present needs. Or perhaps a more accurate statement is that the well-educated appreciate more fully how important a good education is.

Shifting the Tax Burden

During the year there has been much discussion about reducing the burden that has been placed on local property to support the schools. Suggestions have been made to shift more of the burden to state governments or to the federal government or both.

To test sentiment in favor of shifting more of the burden to the state government, this question was asked:

It has been suggested that state taxes be increased for everyone in order to let the state government pay a greater share of school expense and to reduce local property taxes. Would you favor an increase in state taxes so that real estate taxes could be lowered on local property?

For	55%
Against	34%
No opinion	11%

The Value-Added Tax

Still another way of helping to finance the public schools of the nation is the value-added tax, much debated in financial circles.

But the value-added tax fails to arouse much enthusiasm at this time, particularly since it is widely regarded as a regressive tax, falling more heavily on lower-income than on higher-income groups.

The question asked was this:

It has been suggested that a new kind of national sales tax, sometimes called a value-added tax, should be adopted to help reduce local property taxes that now support public schools. Do you favor or oppose such a tax?

Results for the nation:

Favor	34%
Oppose	51%
No opinion	15%

Are New School Buildings More Expensive Than They Need Be?

A majority of citizens (53%) agree that new schools are more expensive than they need be. Thirty-five percent take the opposite view; 12% have no opinion. The professional educators interviewed agreed with the majority viewpoint but by a narrower margin.

To shed light on the public's thinking about building costs, verbatim comments were recorded. They reveal the wide variety of reasons why the public believes that new schools are too expensive:

"I think they are putting too much fancy stuff in these new schools that kids don't need and don't appreciate."

"Far too much goes to architects for designing frills and not enough for basic needs."

"School boards want to build monuments. They forget that changes are going on all the time in education and that schools built today will be obsolete in 20 years. Why not build for 20 years instead of a century?"

"Unfortunately, schools are designed by people who make more money by making them elaborate; they are not designed by those who use them."

"The cost per foot of floor space for new schools here is higher than the cost of good office space. This proves to me that there is graft."

"Why not temporary and portable buildings? These can satisfy educational needs. All you need is a roof over your head and four walls."

"Our schools have a lot of things they don't need: rooms where teachers sit and smoke, wall-to-wall carpeting, air conditioners when the schools are not used in summer."

Those who hold the opposite view — that new school buildings are not too expensive — express their views in these typical comments:

"The extras spent on buildings are a good investment.

They make the kids proud of their school."

"Poor children need to spend part of their day in nice surroundings. The extras spent on buildings are good for their morale."

"Part of the process of education depends on physical environment. In this respect beautiful buildings are important."

"Because of inflation and high construction costs, all buildings built today are too expensive."

Tenure

Increasingly, the public disapproves of the idea of tenure for teachers. As the salaries of educators become comparable with those in other fields, as teachers through their unions and similar organizations develop more clout, and as the supply of teachers begins to exceed the demand, public pressure to give up tenure will almost certainly intensify.

In the present survey, here is how the nation votes on the issue of tenure, as stated in these words:

Most public school teachers have tenure, that is, after a two- or three-year trial period, they receive what amounts to a lifetime contract. Do you approve or disapprove of this policy?

The results for the nation and for two key groups are as follows:

Do you approve or disapprove of tenure?

	National Survey %	Parents of School Children %	Professional Educators %
Approve	28	27	53
Disapprove	61	64	42
No opinion	11	9	5

Two years ago, in the 1970 CFK Ltd. survey, a substantially similar question produced these results: In favor of tenure, 35%; opposed, 53%; no opinion, 12%.

Placing the Blame
For Poor School Work

When a child does poorly in school, who or what is chiefly to blame? The consensus: the child's home life.

To try to find out where the typical citizen places the blame for school failure, this question was asked of all those who participated in the survey, including the professional educators:

> When some children do poorly in school, some people place the blame on the children, some on the children's home life, some on the school, and some on the teachers. Of course, all of these things share the blame, but where would you place the *chief blame*?

The results below show how the nation votes and how this compares with the vote of parents with children now in public school and with the vote of the professional educators.

	National Survey %	Parents of School Children %	Professional Educators %
On the children	14	20	8
On the children's home life	57	53	67
On the school	6	7	9
On the teachers	12	13	7

With such wide agreement that home factors are responsible for educational failure, one wonders why so little attention is being given to the solution of this problem. Neither the schools nor the teachers can be expected to re-order the home life of children, yet many surveys have shown that parents are eager for help and suggestions. This is true of the highly educated as well as the poorly educated. Certainly, if a child's success in school is largely dependent upon his home life, more time and effort should be devoted to finding out ways to deal with these home factors.

Parent-School Liaison

Many schools are now making an effort to bridge the gap

between school and home but their efforts are often casual and misdirected.

Only slightly more than a third of the parents with children enrolled in the public schools had attended any meeting (from September, 1971, through April, 1972) whose purpose was to show how they, as parents, can increase the interest of their children in school work, teach them how and when to do school work, and help in other ways to promote school success.

Year-Around Schools

The proposal that schools be kept open the year around is gaining acceptance throughout the nation. When parents discover that this plan need not interfere with family vacations, some of the opposition is removed.

The percentage of citizens favoring the year-around plan has now reached a clear majority. This question was asked in the latest survey:

> To utilize school buildings to the full extent, would you favor keeping the school open year around? Each student would attend school for nine months over the course of a year. Do you approve or disapprove?

For the nation, the results show:

Approve	53%
Disapprove	41%
No opinion	6%

The professional educator group is even more favorably inclined towards this proposal, as revealed by the following figures:

Approve	66%
Disapprove	30%
No opinion	4%

The trend in favor of the year-around concept is evidenced by comparing the 1970 figures with the present. In the survey two years ago, a total of 42% of the nation's adults approved, 49% disapproved, and 9% had no opinion.

Making School More Interesting

Most parents say their children like to go to school. At the same time they have many ideas about how to make school more interesting. Here, in their verbatim comments, are some of their suggestions:

"Teachers could try much harder to interest students in the subjects they teach. Children can't judge how important something is. They must be told — and sold."

"I have found that if a teacher is enthusiastic about his subject the students will also be enthusiastic. And you can be sure if he isn't the students will be bored."

"More field trips, extra work, doing things they enjoy doing. You learn by doing."

"More discipline is needed to control the hoodlum element. Students can't be expected to learn when the school is in a state of chaos."

"There should be better communication between the teacher and the parent in order to make the parent more effective. The parent could then show more interest in the work the child is doing, and the child, as a result, would take more interest in school."

"My recipe would be to give more responsibility to the student and to select livelier teachers."

"Give the students more study freedom, better access to books. Let students decide what their interests are and then encourage them to follow up these interests."

"Some teachers are just plain boring. There should be some way to reward, with higher salaries, those who are able to interest students."

"Since sports have been cut out of our schools to save money, my son has lost interest in the school and in his work."

"Keep up the creative challenge all the time. School should expect more of every student — the poor as well as the good."

"In this community the kids are afraid to go to school. The bullies and problem makers should be put together and not allowed to bother other students."

"Schools should plan a whole series of special talks to get students to understand and appreciate the importance of what the school is trying to teach them."

Starting Age for School

The proposal that young children start school at the age of 4 does not arouse much enthusiasm from the American public at this time.

Interesting differences are found among different groups, however, as revealed in the percentages below:

Some educators have proposed that young children start school a year earlier — at the age of 4. Does this sound like a good idea or not?

	National %	Parents of Public School Children %	Parents of Private School Children %	Profes- sional Educators %
Favor	32	32	41	40
Oppose	64	65	58	54
No opinion	4	3	`1	6

Compulsory Attendance

A growing viewpoint among professional educators is that it makes little sense to require students to attend school when they are totally uninterested, get little of value from their school work, and all too often become a disrupting factor for other students.

This view, the findings reveal, is largely confined to educators. The public still thinks of the schools in a custodial sense. This question was asked:

In each state children are required to go to school until they reach a certain age. If you were the one to decide, what would be the age in this state? Do you believe those youngsters not interested in school should be forced to attend elementary school (grades 1-6)? Junior and senior high school (grades 7-12)?

The public and the professional educators vote this way:

Leave School at Age:	Public %	Professional Educators %
14 years	2	7
15 years	1	3

16 years	28	42
17 years	11	8
18 years	42	23
19 years	8	4
No minimum age	—	4

Compulsory attendance at elementary school is universally approved. The public votes 91% in favor of this policy.

Compulsory attendance at junior and senior high school is also favored, by 73% in the case of the public, by 56% in the case of professional educators.

Making Better Use of Outside Opportunities

The public likes the idea of permitting students to make greater use of educational opportunities found outside the school. Professional educators are even more in favor of the idea.

This is the question:

In most communities students can learn many things outside the school. Would you approve or disapprove if the schools here reduced the amount of classroom instruction to allow students to make greater use of the educational opportunities outside the school?

The results:

	Public %	Professional Educators %
Approve	56	72
Disapprove	35	26
No opinion	9	2

Least enthusiastic about the idea are the parents with children now enrolled in the public schools. They vote in favor of the idea but by a narrower margin — 49% to 43%.

Nongraded Schools

The public approves of the nongraded school concept by the very substantial margin of 71% to 22%, with 7% expressing no opinion. Professional educators interviewed approve nongraded schools by the ratio of 87% to 11%.

The question asked was this:

> Should a student be able to progress through the school system at his own speed and without regard to the usual grade levels? This would mean that he might study seventh-grade math but only fifth-grade English. Would you favor or oppose such a plan in the local schools?

Approval of this idea is so high throughout the nation that the movement toward nongraded schools will undoubtedly accelerate over the next decade.

Attitudes Toward Local School Boards

Nationally, school boards get high marks from the public for their efforts to improve the quality of education. And those who are in the best position to know — parents who have children now enrolled in the public schools and professional educators — give them the highest marks.

This question was put to those included in the present survey:

> Now, a question about the local school board. . . . Does it work hard to improve the quality of education?

The national result is:

Yes	59%
No	19%
No opinion	22%

The professional educators, in response to the same question, say:

Yes	67%
No	25%
No opinion	8%

In the case of parents with children now attending public schools, the vote is:

Yes	66%
No	21%
No opinion	13%

Teaching as a Career

The public's high regard for teachers and for the teaching profession has been evidenced in many ways in these annual surveys. In the present study, two out of every three citizens interviewed said they would like to have a child of theirs take up teaching as a career. The vote:

Yes	67%
No	22%
No opinion	11%

While this percentage is very high, it is worth noting that it was higher in earlier surveys. Comments by those interviewed shed light on the drop. Many are aware that teaching jobs are scarce and that supply in many areas exceeds demand. Another reason, frequently voiced, is that teaching has become "dangerous," with children permitted to run "wild" in many schools.

The Major Problems

What do you think are the biggest problems with which the *public* schools in this community must deal?

	National Totals	No Children In Schools	Public School Parents	Private School Parents	Professional Educators
	N= 1,790	996	698	144	270
	%	%	%	%	%
Discipline	23	23	23	26	20
Integration/ segregation	18	20	14	17	23
Finances	19	17	22	16	35
Teachers	14	14	14	16	13
Facilities	5	4	7	4	11
Curriculum	5	4	5	4	12

(Continued on next page)

Parents' lack of interest	6	6	6	3	18
Large school, large classes	10	9	10	15	5
Dope, drugs	4	4	4	3	11
There are no problems	2	3	2	2	8
Miscellaneous	9	8	11	12	12
Don't know/ no answer	12	13	12	9	4

What's Right With the Schools

In your opinion, in what ways are your local *public* schools particularly good?

	National Totals	No Children In Schools	Public School Parents	Private School Parents	Profes- sional Educators
N=	1,790	996	698	144	270
	%	%	%	%	%
Teachers	19	15	28	13	29
Curriculum	21	16	28	15	42
Facilities	8	7	9	8	16
Up-to-date teaching method	5	4	8	6	12
Extra curricular activities	5	3	8	8	6
No racial conflicts	7	7	6	4	11
Small school-small classes	3	2	5	1	4
Good administration	3	2	5	3	6
Good student/ teacher relationships	4	2	6	4	6
Parents are interested, participate	2	1	3	3	3
Discipline	2	1	2	–	2
Transportation system		1	1	2	1
Equal opportunities for all	8	8	8	7	19
Close to home	1	1	2	3	1
Nothing is good	7	7	6	15	5
Miscellaneous	1	1	1	–	1
Don't know/ no answer	33	43	19	35	5

Student Rights and Privileges

Generally speaking, do the local public school students in this community have too many rights and privileges, or not enough?

	National Totals	No Children In Schools	Public School Parents	Private School Parents	Professional Educators
	N=1,790	996	698	144	270
	%	%	%	%	%
Too many	41	41	40	40	33
Not enough	11	12	9	12	17
Just right	33	28	42	28	42
No opinion	15	19	9	20	8
	100	100	100	100	100

Rights of Older Students.

Should students who are 18 years of age, and now have the right to vote, have more rights and privileges than other students?

	National Totals	No Children In Schools	Public School Parents	Private School Parents	Professional Educators
	N=1,790	996	698	144	270
	%	%	%	%	%
Yes	21	24	17	19	24
No	73	71	77	76	73
Don't know	6	5	6	5	3
	100	100	100	100	100

School Starting Age

Some educators have proposed that young children start school a year earlier — at the age of 4. Does this sound like a good idea or not?

	National Totals	No Children In Schools	Public School Parents	Private School Parents	Professional Educators
N=	1,790	996	698	144	270
	%	%	%	%	%
Good idea	32	31	32	41	40
Poor idea	64	64	65	58	54
No opinion	4	5	3	1	6
	100	100	100	100	100

Same question, answers by other categories.

	Percent Totals	Good Idea %	Poor Idea %	Don't Know/ No Answer %
Sex				
Men	100	33	63	4
Women	100	31	65	4
Race				
White	100	28	68	4
Nonwhite	100	63	34	3
Education				
Elementary grades	100	24	72	4
High school incomplete	100	29	67	4
High school complete	100	34	63	3
Technical, trade, or business school	100	38	61	1
College incomplete	100	37	56	7
College graduate	100	33	63	4
Occupation				
Business & professional	100	33	61	6
Clerical & sales	100	42	56	2
Farm	100	14	82	4
Skilled labor	100	29	69	2
Unskilled labor	100	36	61	3
Non-labor force	100	27	68	5
Age				
Under 21 years	100	39	54	7
21 to 29 years	100	47	51	2
30 to 49 years	100	32	64	4
50 years and over	100	24	72	4
Religion				
Protestant	100	28	69	3
Roman Catholic	100	33	63	4
Jewish	100	54	34	12
All others	100	48	46	6
Region				
East	100	36	59	5
Midwest	100	28	70	2
South	100	29	68	3
West	100	37	59	4
Income				
$15,000 and over	100	34	62	4
$10,000 to $14,999	100	36	61	3
$ 7,000 to $ 9,999	100	30	67	3
$ 5,000 to $ 6,999	100	33	62	5
$ 3,000 to $ 4,999	100	29	67	4
Under $3,000	100	23	72	5

500,000 and over	100	45	49	6
50,000 to 499,999	100	33	64	3
25,000 to 49,999	100	29	67	4
Under 25,000	100	22	75	3

Teacher Tenure

Most public school teachers have tenure; that is, after a two- or three-year trial period, they receive what amounts to a lifetime contract. Do you approve or disapprove of this policy?

	National Totals	No Children In Schools	Public School Parents	Private School Parents	Profes- sional Educators
N=	1,790	996	698	144	270
	%	%	%	%	%
Approve	28	28	27	28	53
Disapprove	61	59	64	63	42
No opinion	11	13	9	9	5
	100	100	100	100	100

Compulsory Attendance, Upper Age Limits

In each state children are required to go to school until they reach a certain age. If you were the one to decide, what would be the age?

	National Totals	No Children In Schools	Public School Parents	Private School Parents	Profes- sional Educators
N=	1,790	996	698	144	270
	%	%	%	%	%
14 years & under	2	2	0	1	7
15 years	1	2	1	1	3
16 years	28	29	28	18	42
Over 16 years	61	60	64	65	35
Don't know	8	7	7	15	9
	100	100	100	100	96*

*Four percent of the professional educators opted for no minimum age; that is, they do not believe in compulsory education.

Same question, answers by other categories.

	Per-cent Totals	14 Yrs. %	15 Yrs. %	16 Yrs. %	Over 16 Yrs. %	Don't Know/ No Answer %
Sex						
Men	100	2	2	31	57	8
Women	100	1	1	26	65	7
Race						
White	100	2	2	30	59	7
Nonwhite	100	1	0	11	77	11
Education						
Elementary grades	100	1	1	28	59	11
High school incom-plete	100	1	1	21	70	7
High school complete	100	1	1	25	67	6
Technical, trade, or business school	100	2	2	35	59	2
College incomplete	100	2	2	36	53	7
College graduate	100	5	3	36	46	10
Occupation						
Business & pro-fessional	100	3	2	33	54	8
Clerical & sales	100	1	2	25	64	8
Farm	100	0	1	26	72	1
Skilled labor	100	1	0	25	66	8
Unskilled labor	100	1	1	23	67	8
Non-labor force	100	2	3	31	56	8
Age						
Under 21 years	100	1	1	29	61	8
21 to 29 years	100	3	1	26	62	8
30 to 49 years	100	1	1	27	63	8
50 years and over	100	2	2	30	61	5
Religion						
Protestant	100	2	1	28	63	6
Roman Catholic	100	1	1	24	67	7
Jewish	100	3	6	35	39	7
All others	100	3	2	37	47	11
Region						
East	100	3	2	28	59	8
Midwest	100	1	1	31	62	5
South	100	1	1	22	67	9
West	100	2	3	32	57	6
Income						
$15,000 and over	100	3	3	35	52	7
$10,000 to $14,999	100	0	1	29	65	5
$ 7,000 to $ 9,999	100	1	0	26	66	7
$ 5,000 to $ 6,999	100	1	1	23	67	8

$ 3,000 to $ 4,999	100	3	2	27	61	6
Under $3,000	100	3	3	25	58	11
Community size						
500,000 and over	100	2	2	24	64	8
50,000 to 499,999	100	2	3	31	59	5
25,000 to 49,999	100	2	0	13	84	1
Under 25,000	100	2	2	30	60	6

Compulsory Attendance, Lower Age Limits

Do you believe those youngsters not interested in school should be forced to attend elementary school (grades 1 to 6)?

	National Totals	No Children In Schools	Public School Parents	Private School Parents	Professional Educators
N=	1,790	996	698	144	270
	%	%	%	%	%
Yes	91	91	92	93	91
No	7	7	7	6	9
Don't know	2	2	1	1	0
	100	100	100	100	100

Junior and senior high school (grades 7 to 12)?

Yes	73	71	75	76	56
No	24	25	23	18	38
Don't know	3	4	2	6	6
	100	100	100	100	100

Voting Tax Increases

Suppose the local *public* schools said they needed much more money. As you feel at this time, would you vote to raise taxes for this purpose. or would you vote against raising taxes for this purpose.

	National Totals	No Children In Schools	Public School Parents	Private School Parents	Professional Educators
N=	1,790	996	698	144	270
	%	%	%	%	%
For	36	35	37	38	67
Against	56	56	56	55	29
No opinion	8	9	7	7	4
	100	100	100	100	100

Same question, answers by other categories.

	Percent Totals	For %	Against %	Don't Know/ No Answer %
Sex				
Men	100	37	56	7
Women	100	35	57	8
Race				
White	100	35	57	8
Nonwhite	100	41	48	11
Education				
Elementary grades	100	27	64	9
High school incomplete	100	32	61	7
High school complete	100	33	60	7
Technical, trade, or business school	100	38	59	3
College incomplete	100	45	45	10
College graduate	100	50	41	9
Occupation				
Business & professional	100	43	50	7
Clerical & sales	100	47	47	6
Farm	100	26	65	9
Skilled labor	100	33	60	7
Unskilled labor	100	30	61	9
Non-labor force	100	30	62	8
Age				
Under 21 years	100	45	42	13
21-29 years	100	41	49	10
30-49 years	100	36	57	7
50 years and older	100	32	61	7
Religion				
Protestant	100	36	57	7
Roman Catholic	100	32	59	9
Jewish	100	55	39	6
All others	100	35	52	13
Region				
East	100	33	58	9
Midwest	100	37	58	5
South	100	37	53	10
West	100	36	55	9
Income				
$15,000 and over	100	39	54	7
$10,000 to $14,999	100	40	52	8
$ 7,000 to $ 9,999	100	34	59	7
$ 5,000 to $ 6,999	100	36	58	6
$ 3,000 to $ 4,999	100	27	64	9
Under $3,000	100	27	58	15

Community size

500,000 and over	100	37	54	9
50,000 to 499,999	100	37	55	8
25,000 to 49,999	100	22	78	0
Under 25,000	100	35	57	8

Higher State Taxes, Lower Property Taxes

It has been suggested that state taxes be increased for everyone in order to let the state government pay a greater share of school expense and to reduce local property taxes. Would you favor an increase in state taxes so that real estate taxes could be lowered on local property?

	National Totals	No Children In Schools	Public School Parents	Private School Parents	Profes-sional Educators
N=	1,790	996	698	144	270
	%	%	%	%	%
For	55	56	54	51	68
Against	34	33	36	37	27
No opinion	11	11	10	12	5
	100	100	100	100	100

Same question, answers by other categories.

	Percent Totals	For %	Against %	Don't Know/ No Answer %
Sex				
Men	100	55	35	10
Women	100	55	33	12
Race				
White	100	55	35	10
Nonwhite	100	56	30	14
Education				
Elementary grades	100	49	35	16
High school incomplete	100	56	34	10
High school complete	100	57	31	12
Technical, trade, or business school	100	48	41	11
College incomplete	100	56	36	8
College graduate	100	58	35	7

(Continued on next page)

Occupation

Business & professional	100	57	35	8
Clerical & sales	100	53	29	18
Farm	100	59	26	15
Skilled labor	100	52	40	8
Unskilled labor	100	58	34	8
Non-labor force	100	52	33	15

Age

Under 21 years	100	63	24	13
21-29 years	100	55	35	10
30-49 years	100	55	35	10
50 years and over	100	54	34	12

Religion

Protestant	100	55	34	11
Roman Catholic	100	57	33	10
Jewish	100	54	37	9
All others	100	49	38	13

Region

East	100	54	35	11
Midwest	100	58	32	10
South	100	48	38	14
West	100	61	31	8

Income

$15,000 and over	100	55	35	10
$10,000 to $14,999	100	54	36	10
$ 7,000 to $ 9,999	100	55	37	8
$ 5,000 to $ 6,999	100	56	32	12
$ 3,000 to $ 4,999	100	60	27	13
Under $3,000	100	51	31	18

Community size

500,000 and over	100	55	33	12
50,000 to 499,999	100	52	36	12
25,000 to 49,999	100	58	36	6
Under 25,000	100	56	34	10

The Value-Added Tax

It has been suggested that a new kind of national sales tax, sometimes called a value-added tax, should be adopted to help reduce local property taxes that now support public schools. Do you favor or oppose such a tax?

	National Totals	No Children In Schools	Public School Parents	Private School Parents	Professional Educators
N=	1,790	996	698	144	270
	%	%	%	%	%
Favor	35	35	30	37	38
Oppose	51	50	54	51	53
No opinion	14	15	16	12	9
	100	100	100	100	100

Increasing the Child's Interest in School

Can anything be done by the school to increase your child's interest in going to school?

	Public School Parents	Private School Parents
N=	698	144
	%	%
Yes	42	30
No	46	51
Don't know	12	19
	100	100

Placing Blame for Poor School Work

When some children do poorly in school, some people place the blame on the children, some on the children's home life, some on the school, and some on the teachers. Of course, all of these things share the blame, but where would you place the *chief* blame?

	National Totals	No Children In Schools	Public School Parents	Private School Parents	Professional Educators
N=	1,790	996	698	144	270
	%	%	%	%	%
On children	14	11	20	12	8
On children's home life	57	61	53	58	67
On schools	6	5	7	10	9
On teachers	12	11	13	12	7
No opinion	13	15	12	14	10

Note: Columns add to more than 100% because of some multiple responses.

Teaching as a Career

Would you like to have a child of yours take up teaching in the public schools as a career?

	National Totals	No Children In Schools	Public School Parents	Private School Parents	Profes- sional Educators
N=	1,790	996	698	144	270
	%	%	%	%	%
Yes	67	65	71	61	72
No	22	21	21	31	22
Don't know	11	14	8	8	6
	100	100	100	100	100

The Nongraded School

Should a student be able to progress through the school system at his own speed and without regard to the usual grade levels? This would mean that he might study seventh-grade math but only fifth-grade English. Would you favor or oppose such a plan in the local schools?

	National Totals	No Children In Schools	Public School Parents	Private School Parents	Profes- sional Educators
N=	1,790	996	698	144	270
	%	%	%	%	%
Favor	71	69	74	73	87
Oppose	22	22	22	22	11
No opinion	7	9	4	5	2
	100	100	100	100	100

The Year-Around School

To utilize school buildings to the full extent, would you favor keeping the school open year around? Each student would attend school for nine months over the course of a year. Do you approve or disapprove?

	National Totals	No Children In Schools	Public School Parents	Private School Parents	Professional Educators
N=	1,790	996	698	144	270
	%	%	%	%	%
Approve	53	56	50	52	66
Disapprove	41	37	47	43	30
Don't know	6	7	3	5	4
	100	100	100	100	100

Parents' Meetings

Have you attended *any* meeting since last September where the chief topic was how you, as a parent, could increase the interest of your child(ren) in his (their) school work, how and when to do homework, and other such matters that show what can be done at home to help the child in school?

	Public School Parents	Private School Parents
N=	698	144
	%	%
Yes	37	41
No	61	56
Can't recall	2	3
	100	100

The School Without Walls

In most communities students can learn many things outside the school. Would you approve or disapprove if the schools here reduced the amount of classroom instruction to allow students to make greater use of the educational opportunities outside the school?

	National Totals	No Children In Schools	Public School Parents	Private School Parents	Professional Educators
N=	1,790	996	698	144	270
	%	%	%	%	%
Approve	56	60	49	63	72

(Continued on next page)

Disapprove	34	29	43	29	26
No opinion	10	11	8	8	2
	100	100	100	100	100

Rating the School Board

Now, a question about the local school board. Does it work hard to improve the quality of education?

	National Totals	No Children In Schools	Public School Parents	Private School Parents	Profes- sional Educators
N=	1,790	996	698	144	270
	%	%	%	%	%
Yes	59	54	66	58	67
No	19	18	21	19	25
No opinion	22	28	13	23	8
	100	100	100	100	100

Analysis of Respondents

National Adults

No children in school	56%
Public school parents	39%*
Parochial and private school parents	8%*

*Totals exceed 44% because some parents have children attending more than one kind of school.

A key element in making comparisons with earlier years is to keep constant the number of persons with *no children in school.* This has been done by a simple weighting process carried out by use of the computer.

Sex	%
Men	48
Women	52
	100
Race	
White	89
Nonwhite	11
	100

Age

18-20 years	5
21-29 years	19
30-49 years	39
50 years and over	37
	100

Religion

Protestant	61
Roman Catholic	26
Jewish	4
Others	9
	100

Region

East	29
Midwest	27
South	26
West	18
	100

Community size

500,000 and over	33
50,000 to 499,999	22
25,000 to 49,999	2
Under 25,000	43
	100

Education

Elementary grades	16
High school incomplete	20
High school complete	32
Technical, trade, or business school	5
College incomplete	14
College graduate	13
	100

Occupation

Business and professional	26
Clerical and sales	11
Farm	5
Skilled labor	17
Unskilled labor	21
Non-labor force	18
Undesignated	2
	100

Income

$15,000 and over	21
$10,000 – $14,999	26
$ 7,000 – $ 9,999	17
$ 5,000 – $ 6,999	15

(Continued on next page)

(Continued from preceding page)

$ 4,000 − $ 4,999	6
$ 3,000 − $ 3,999	5
Under $2,999	8
Undesignated	2
	100

Chapter 6
Fifth Annual Gallup Poll of Public Attitudes Toward Education

Purpose of the Study

The survey reported in the following pages was sponsored by CFK Ltd. and is the fifth in an annual series designed to measure and record the attitude of American citizens toward their public schools.

Each year new areas are covered as new problems come forth. Some questions are repeated from earlier years in order to measure trends.

The findings of this study apply to the nation as a whole and not necessarily to any single community. These findings do, however, permit local communities to compare results of surveys conducted within their own community with the results of the national survey.

The study represents the joint planning of the staff of CFK Ltd. and the staff of Gallup International. Valuable help in selection of the areas of interests and concern to be included in the survey came from: Medill Bair, superintendent of schools, Hartford, Conn. (now director, Educational Collaboratory of Greater Boston, Harvard University); B. Frank Brown, director, Information and Services, I/D/E/A, Melbourne, Fla.; George L. Brown, state senator, Colorado, and executive director, Metro Denver Urban Coalition; Stanley Elam, editor, *Phi Delta Kappan,* Bloomington, Ind.; Richard Koeppe, superintendent, Cherry Creek School District No. 5, Englewood, Colo.; Etta Lee Powell, principal, North Bethesda Junior High School,

Bethesda, Md.; Donald Waldrip, superintendent of schools, Cincinnati, O.

Research Procedure

The Sample. The sample embraced a total of 1,627 adults. It is described as a modified probability sample of the nation. Interviewing was conducted in every area of the country and in all types of communities. These communities, taken together, represent a true microcosm of the nation. A full description of the adult sample will be found at the end of this report.

A separate survey was undertaken to learn the views of professional educators. This sample embraced 306 educators (teachers, assistant principals, principals, administrators, superintendents). These persons also were interviewed in every area of the country and in all types of communities.

The Interviewing Form. Questions included in the questionnaire were selected after several pretests conducted by the field staff maintained by the Gallup organizations.

Time of Interviewing. The field work for this study was conducted during the period of May 11 through 13, 1973.

Major Problems Confronting The Public Schools in 1973

When the public is asked to name the most important problems confronting the public schools in their community, discipline leads the list — as it has four out of the last five years.

There has been a slight change, however. The percentage of respondents naming discipline is not quite so high as it was in 1969, a period of turmoil in the colleges and universities. But rising in the list, and now in second place, is the complex of problems arising from integration/segregation. Five years ago these racial issues were fifth on the list of problems.

In the 1969 survey, the use of drugs by students was mentioned by very few. In the 1973 survey, drug use is mentioned by enough respondents to place it fifth in the list of problems. In 1969 lack of proper school facilities was second in the list; now this problem has dropped to ninth place.

Problems do change, it can be seen, even in a relatively short period of time. Unfortunately, the two problems which head the list today — discipline and racial disorder — are the very stuff from which front-page newspaper articles are born. This bad publicity has had a marked influence on the public, as survey results show, and especially on those persons who do not have children in the schools and who must rely to a greater extent, therefore, on the media for their information about the public schools.

Here is the list of problems confronting the public schools, in order of mentions for 1973:

1. Lack of discipline
2. Integration/segregation problems
3. Lack of proper financial support
4. Difficulty of getting "good" teachers
5. Use of drugs
6. Size of school/classes
7. Poor curriculum
8. Parents' lack of interest
9. Lack of proper facilities
10. School board policies

When professional educators were asked the same question, their replies in general agree with the public's, with a few notable differences. For example, lack of proper financial support rates as the number one problem with this group, and the lack of good teachers number eight. The educators would include pupils' lack of interest along with parents' lack of interest among the top 10 problems.

In What Ways Are the Local Public Schools Particularly Good?

Having directed the thinking of respondents to the problems — to what is wrong with the public schools — it was only proper to ask those included in the survey to tell what they thought was right. Here are their answers, listed in order of mentions:

1. The curriculum
2. The teachers
3. School facilities
4. Extracurricular activities
5. Up-to-date teaching methods
6. Absence of racial conflicts
7. Good administration

Professional educators name the good points about the public schools in about this same order. They head their list with "good teachers" and place both up-to-date teaching methods and good administration higher on their lists.

In an earlier survey report the absence of objective criteria in judging the public schools was noted. The same observation holds for the present study. Factors that would be important in a program of accountability are seldom, if ever, mentioned.

Changes of Attitude in Recent Years

Included in the present survey was one of the most revealing questions asked in this series of annual surveys:

In recent years has your overall attitude toward the *public* schools in your community become more favorable or less favorable?

Replies to this question, and analysis of the reasons why respondents feel more favorably or less favorably toward the schools, reveal a basic fact: The more respondents know at firsthand about the public schools, the more favorable are their views; the less interested and less well informed, the less favorable. Most important is the fact that persons who depend on the media for their information are most critical of the schools.

Parents with children now in the public schools say they have become more favorable in their views of the public schools in recent years; those who have no children in school hold the reverse opinion.

Professional educators are about evenly divided between those whose views have become more favorable and those whose views have become less favorable.

Here are the results by groups:

	National Totals	No Children In Schools	Public School Parents	Private School Parents	Professional Educators
N=	1,627	928	620	124	306
	%	%	%	%	%
Attitudes Toward Schools					
Becoming more favorable	32	25	42	31	39
Becoming less favorable	36	38	31	46	41
No change/ no opinion	32	37	27	23	20
	100	100	100	100	100

It can be argued that, of the groups named above, the best judge of the public schools should be the parents of children who are now attending these schools. And the weight of their opinion is clearly on the favorable side.

From this, it might be assumed that an information program that gives the public a better idea of what the schools are doing, and trying to do, would have an important impact on the general public's views.

Sources of Information About the Schools

For the general public, the best source of information about the public schools in their communities is the students themselves. Of the media, the best source of information is clearly the newspapers. The broadcast media — radio and television — are cited by only half as many.

Parents of students rank second as a source of information, with teachers and the school board receiving the same number of mentions. What the survey findings seem to indicate, therefore, is that attitudes about the quality of the local schools are based upon information gained from many sources: the firsthand experience of students and teachers and from other parents, as well as from the media of communication, especially newspapers. The question:

What are the sources of information you use to judge the quality of schools in your community; that is, where do you get your information about the schools?

The results:

	National Totals	No Children In Schools	Public School Parents	Private School Parents	Profes- sional Educators
N=	1,627	928	620	124	306
	%	%	%	%	%
Sources of Information					
Students	43	35	56	48	48
Newspapers	38	42	33	41	34
School board/ faculty	33	24	45	46	82
Parents of students	33	31	35	41	39
Other adults in community	23	24	22	20	27
Radio and/or television	20	25	14	18	21
Other	12	12	13	15	20
PTA	3	--	7	5	1
Undesignated	4	6	2	2	1

(Totals exceed 100% because of multiple responses.)

Discipline

Because discipline so regularly leads the public's list of "problems" of the public schools, an attempt was made to probe into the meaning attached to this word by the public. Respondents were therefore asked this open-ended question:

When we talk about "discipline" in the schools, just what does this mean to you?

The following statements convey some idea of the wide range of views:

"Discipline is respect for the teacher on the part of the child; and respect for the child on the part of the teacher."

"Learning taking place without confusion."

"Keeping children so interested in what they are learning that obeying the rules is almost automatic."

"Discipline is self-control and a proper respect for other students, for those in authority."

"Without discipline neither school nor society can exist. The world would be bedlam."

"Proper discipline makes children happier. When they run wild, they are undone by the confusion they create."

Most respondents see discipline as a matter of obeying rules, respecting views of parents, teachers, and others in authority, and being considerate of fellow students who wish to learn in a peaceful atmosphere.

While law and order have become almost code words for the conservative viewpoint in politics, the basic concept is held in high regard by the public. In fact, in the 1972 survey, when asked to choose from a list of nine goals of education, the public placed "teaching students to respect law and authority" as the top goal for students in grades 7-12.

Are High Schools Getting Too Large?

In the 1950s James Conant argued persuasively that high schools should be large because only the large high schools could afford to have special courses in special subjects, since small high schools would not have enough students interested in these fields to warrant separate classes.

Apparently the tide has turned. Today all groups, including professional educators, are of the opinion that schools are too large; only a relatively small percentage hold that they are not big enough.

The ideal size of a school usually gets related in the typical person's mind to the size of school that he attended. To minimize this factor, a question was designed that sought to remove the issue at least one step from the respondent's own experience. The question that proved best, after testing, is as follows:

In some areas of the U.S., new towns and cities are being built. This gives city planners the opportunity to build school facilities that are "just right" in size.

What do you think would be the "ideal" number of students in a high school?

After this question was asked, a second question sought to elicit opinions on the general issue of whether high schools are too large or not large enough. Replies to the latter question show that major groups making up the public agree quite closely. Professional educators show even a larger proportion holding the view that schools are too large.

Here is the question:

Do you think high schools today are getting too large or aren't they large enough?

	National Totals	No Children In Schools	Public School Parents	Private School Parents	Profes- sional Educators
N=	1,627	928	620	124	306
	%	%	%	%	%
Getting too large	57	55	60	61	76
Not large enough	13	12	14	12	5
Just right	15	15	15	15	9
No opinion	15	18	11	12	9
	100	100	100	100	99*

*Where sum of percentages in columns does not total 100%, it is due to rounding of the figures.

When the views of all persons who gave a figure which represented, for them, the ideal size of a high school in a "new city," the median figure turns out to be 500.

Does Class Size Make a Difference?

While recent research findings point to the fact that, within certain limits, size of class makes little difference in student achievement, the general public is still convinced that smaller classes make "a great deal of difference" — a view shared by the professional educators who participated in this survey.

Every major group in the population holds the belief that student achievement is related to class size. The question asked respondents was this:

> In some school districts, the typical class has as many as 35 students; in other districts, only 20. In regard to the achievement or progress of students, do you think small classes make a great deal of difference, little difference, or no difference at all?

	National Totals	No Children In Schools	Public School Parents	Private School Parents	Professional Educators
N=	1,627	928	620	124	306
	%	%	%	%	%
A great deal of difference	79	75	83	87	85
Little difference	11	11	11	7	11
No difference	6	8	4	4	1
No opinion	4	6	2	2	2
	100	100	100	100	99*

*Due to rounding

Money Spent Related to Student Achievement

Just as some studies have shown that student achievement is not closely related to class size, so other studies have shown that the amount of money spent per child on his education — again within certain limits — bears little relationship to the child's progress in school. Since this research will almost certainly be a factor in future consideration of the financial needs of the public schools, it is important to discover how the public feels on this issue. Is quality of education closely correlated in the public's thinking with the amount a school district spends on the educational program per child?

The answers bring to light a number of interesting differences between the general public and the educators — and reveal some inconsistency in the thinking of the average citizen on this matter.

Professional educators say that the additional expenditure of money per child makes a "great difference." The public is evenly divided as to whether it makes a "great difference" or "little difference." If those who answer "no difference" are added to those who say "little difference," then a plurality of the public could be said to hold the view that additional expenditures by school districts make little or no difference. And yet these same respondents, in a related question, held that small classes were important to educational quality and to student achievement.

What this means, it seems reasonable to assume, is that the public has not yet connected school expenditures per child to class size.

The question was stated in this fashion:

In some school districts, about $600 is spent per child per school year; some school districts spend more than $1,200. Do you think this additional expenditure of money makes a great deal of difference in the achievement or progress of students — or little difference?

Here are the answers:

	National Totals	No Children In Schools	Public School Parents	Private School Parents	Professional Educators
N=	1,627	928	620	124	306
	%	%	%	%	%
Great deal of difference	39	35	45	40	59
Little difference	38	39	36	39	25
No difference	10	11	8	10	6
Don't know	13	15	11	11	10
	100	100	100	100	100

State Financial Help to Schools

The suggestion that state governments increase taxes to pay more of the cost of local schools is voted down by the public by a 5:4 ratio. Professional educators, on the other hand, like the idea, and cast a vote of more than 2 to 1 in favor of the proposal.

In last year's survey it was discovered that if a definite promise is made that local property taxes will be reduced, the public would favor shifting more of the costs of operating the local schools to the state government. But without such a promise, the public opposes the plan.

The question this year was stated as follows:

It has been suggested that state government through increased taxes pay more of the cost of local school expenses. Would you favor or oppose an increase in state taxes for this purpose?

	National Totals	No Children In Schools	Public School Parents	Private School Parents	Professional Educators
N=	1,627	928	620	124	306
	%	%	%	%	%
Favor increase	40	38	44	41	65
Oppose increase	50	51	49	52	29
No opinion	10	11	7	7	6
	100	100	100	100	100

The 1972 question was:

It has been suggested that state taxes be increased for everyone in order to let the state government pay a greater share of school expense and to reduce local property taxes. Would you favor an increase in state taxes so that real estate taxes could be lowered on local property?

The results:

	National Totals	No Children In Schools	Public School Parents	Private School Parents	Professional Educators
N=	1,790	996	698	144	270
	%	%	%	%	%
For	55	56	54	51	68
Against	34	33	36	37	27
No opinion	11	11	10	12	5
	100	100	100	100	100

Satisfaction with Curriculum

Parents of school children — both those whose children are now attending the public schools and those with children in private or parochial schools — say they are satisfied with their children's courses. When asked if their sons and daughters are "learning the things you believe [they] should," more than eight in 10 parents of children in the public schools say yes. Parents with children in private or independent schools express their satisfaction at an even higher level.

The question:

Now, thinking about your oldest child in school (elementary, junior or senior high — not college): Do you think he (she) is learning the things you believe he (she) should be learning?

	National Totals	Public School Parents	Private School Parents
N=	699	620	124
	%	%	%
Yes	82	81	86
No	13	14	10
Don't know	5	5	4
	100	100	100

A second question asked if the child (the oldest one in public school) is happy going to school, or whether he (or she) attends school simply because he (she) is required to do so. Equally high percentages of parents say yes to this question. Only one parent in seven (14%) reports that the child in question goes to school only because he must. These results need to be interpreted carefully. There are many degrees of liking; if a parent does not meet active resistance from the child, he is likely to assume that the child likes school.

But even taking the results at face value, the fact that one child in seven goes to school only because he is required to presents a major problem for the schools, especially if children in this category are disruptive and the source of many discipline problems.

The question:

Is he (she) happy to go to school — that is, does he (she) go to school because he (she) wants to go or simply because he (she) is required to attend?

	National Totals	Public School Parents	Private School Parents
N=	699	620	124
	%	%	%
Wants to go	83	83	83
Goes because it is required	14	15	12
No opinion	3	2	5
	100	100	100

More Emphasis to Career Education

Few proposals receive such overwhelming approval today as the suggestion that schools give more emphasis to a study of trades, professions, and businesses to help students decide on their careers. Nine in 10 persons in all major groups sampled in this survey say they would like to have the schools give more emphasis to this part of the educational program.

And most of those who vote for this greater emphasis say that this program should start with junior and senior high school, although many professional educators think it should start even earlier — in the elementary grades.

The question:

Should public schools give more emphasis to a study of trades, professions, and businesses to help students decide on their careers?

	National Totals	No Children In School	Public School Parents	Private School Parents	Profes- sional Educators
N=	1,627	928	620	124	306
	%	%	%	%	%
Yes, more emphasis	90	90	90	89	90
No	7	7	7	9	9
No opinion	3	3	3	2	1
	100	100	100	100	100

Alternative Schools

The surveys conducted in this five-year series have indicated that the public is usually sympathetic to new educational ideas, especially if these innovations represent a solution, in whole or in part, to a situation that needs correcting. The public's attitude can be summed up in a statement which comes frequently from respondents who are being asked to express their views on a new proposal: "Something must be done and nothing will be lost in giving this [plan or proposal] a try."

The American public, it has been found in countless surveys, is pragmatic. If a plan works, that's fine; if it doesn't, get rid of it. And the people want to be the judge as to whether or not it works.

Throughout the nation the press reports the difficulties schools are having with racial problems, school dropouts, discipline, and juvenile delinquency; the public is ready to try any solution that gives hope in solving these problems. One of the solutions is the alternative school, and the public seems ready to give it a try — and to judge later how well it works.

The plans now being tried in various areas of the nation all vary in some manner; for this reason the question put to the public in describing the alternative school had to be stated in a very generalized form. It was stated as follows:

For students who are not interested in, or are bored with, the usual kind of education, it has been proposed that new kinds of local schools be established. They usually place more responsibility upon the student for what he learns and how he learns it. Some use the community as their laboratory and do not use the usual kind of classrooms. Do you think this is a good idea or a poor idea?

	National Totals	No Children In Schools	Public School Parents	Private School Parents	Professional Educators
N=	1,627	928	620	124	306
	%	%	%	%	%
Good idea	62	62	62	61	80
Poor idea	26	24	28	27	15
No opinion	12	14	10	12	5
	100	100	100	100	100

From the above table it can be seen that professional educators, who are much more familiar with this idea than the general public, give it an even higher vote of approval.

Parents' Right To Sue

At least one suit has been filed against a U.S. school district by the parents of a student who had not been taught to read after a number of years in school.

The question arises as to whether the public believes that some kind of accountability should be imposed by legal action.

Fortunately, at least for those in charge of school financing, the public votes no on this issue by a substantial majority. Least in favor, as one might expect, are professional educators, who vote the suggestion down 5-1.

However, if even one parent in 100 holds to this view, future trouble may be in store for the schools. Parents of children now in the public schools vote 28% in favor of this idea to 64% against.

The question:

Do you think parents should have the right to sue a school district if a student of normal intelligence and without physical disabilities reaches the sixth grade without being able to read?

	National Totals	No Children In School	Public School Parents	Private School Parents	Profes- sional Educators
	N= 1,627	928	620	124	306
	%	%	%	%	%
Yes, should have right	27	26	28	35	16
No	64	65	64	60	80
No opinion	9	9	8	5	4
	100	100	100	100	100

Attitudes Toward School Integration

Professional educators and parents with one or more children now attending public school are more inclined than other respondents to say that not enough is being done to integrate the schools throughout the nation.

While the overall vote shows slightly more holding the view that less should be done to integrate the schools, it is worth noting that attitudes toward integration are far less antagonistic than attitudes toward busing. The two — integration and busing — should not be confused. While busing is one way to bring about integration, polls have consistently shown an overwhelming majority of Americans opposed to achieving integration in this manner. Far too many persons considering this problem confuse ends with means.

The question asked:

Now, a question about how you feel about school integration. Do you believe more should be done — or less should be done — to integrate the schools throughout the nation?

	National Totals	No Children In School	Public School Parents	Private School Parents	Profes- sional Educators
N=	1,627	928	620	124	306
	%	%	%	%	%
More should be done	30	29	31	26	41
Less should be done	38	40	36	36	29
No change from present	23	21	25	27	22
No opinion	9	10	8	11	8
	100	100	100	100	100

All respondents were asked if they felt differently about integration now than they did a few years ago. Most said their views hadn't changed; only one person in six said he had changed his views in recent years. When the views of persons in this group are examined, responses show a slight change against integration.

Should Children Start School at Age 4?

The proposal to have children start school at age 4 arises with increasing frequency. Such a plan would, according to some authorities, make it possible to end schooling at the age of 17 for the typical student, thus permitting him to go to work or enter college a year earlier. But generally it is defended on other grounds.

The proposal still does not meet with majority approval on the part of the public — or, for that matter, of professional educators.

Moreover, there is no survey evidence to indicate a trend in the direction of support for such a plan. In the survey conducted in 1972, the vote in favor of this proposal was 32%, with 64% opposed and 4% with no opinion. Comparable figures for this year are: 30% in favor, 64% opposed, and 6% with no opinion.

The question:

Some educators have proposed that children start school one year earlier, that is, at age 4. Would you approve or disapprove of such a plan in this community?

	National Totals	No Children In School	Public School Parents	Private School Parents	Profes- sional Educators
	N= 1,627	928	620	124	306
	%	%	%	%	%
Favor	30	29	31	40	32
Oppose	64	64	64	55	63
No opinion	6	7	5	5	5
	100	100	100	100	100

In private schools, where the practice of starting children at age 4 is more common, the idea of introducing this plan in the public schools receives a higher approval vote.

Why Do Families Move to the Suburbs?

One of the most pronounced changes in America is the continued shift of population from the inner cities to the suburbs. Are the residents of big cities moving to suburbia because of the schools, the crime and drug problems, or what? If it is primarily to obtain a better education, then, in theory at least, the shift in population might be halted by improvement in the quality of city schools.

To discover the reasons, an open question was framed that offered respondents freedom to answer in terms of the motivations of other people, but which actually can be presumed to fit their own thinking.

Interestingly, education does not emerge as the prime motive. In fact, it is relatively far down the list, even with parents of school children.

The reasons most often cited for this population shift largely concern congestion — the desire to escape to places less affected by the pollution and crowded living conditions found in large cities.

Other studies have shown that the century-old trend from country to city has been reversed, and that the public not only wants to move from large cities to suburban areas, but from medium-size cities to smaller cities, and from smaller cities to the open countryside.

Parents of children now in the public schools give the following reasons for the shift from the big cities to the suburban communities, listed in order of mention:

1. Congestion/noise/pollution
2. Fear of crime
3. To get away from minorities
4. More desirable housing
5. Better educational opportunities

Professional educators, on the other hand, rate education higher on their list of reasons why people are moving from the big cities to the suburbs.

The Importance of Education to Success

For decades the American public has regarded education as the royal road to success. There is little evidence that this attitude is changing, despite some current theories that genetics and home environment are the controlling factors. The group that shows most evidence of growing doubt is the group made up of professional educators. Some of their disillusionment can be explained, perhaps, by the lack of interest on the part of some students who stay in school only because the law requires it.

The question:

How important are schools to one's future suc-

cess — extremely important, fairly important, not too important?

	National Totals	No Children In School	Public School Parents	Private School Parents	Professional Educators
N=	1,627	928	620	124	306
	%	%	%	%	%
Extremely important	76	71	81	84	69
Fairly important	19	22	16	13	28
Not too important	4	5	2	2	2
No opinion	1	2	--	1	1
	100	100	99*	100	100

*Due to rounding

When asked if their feelings had changed over the years about the importance of education, only one in five replied in the affirmative. However, in the case of professional educators the proportion is nearly three in 10, and among this group the majority feel that education is *less important* today. By contrast, fewer members of the general public say their views on the importance of education have changed. Of those whose views have changed, the great majority say it has been to *strengthen* their belief in education as a key to one's future success.

Is Education Better or Worse Than in Your Day?

Solid agreement is registered by all groups on the question of whether children today get a better education than their parents did. The answer is "better" by a substantial margin. Those who are in a position to be best informed — those parents who have one or more children in the public schools — vote more than 3 to 1 that schools are better today than in their time. Even those who report that in *recent* years their attitudes have become less favorable are still inclined to say that the schools are better than they were when they attended.

The question:

As you look on your own elementary and high school education, is it your impression that children today get a better — or worse — education than you did?

	National Totals	No Children In School	Public School Parents	Private School Parents	Professional Educators
N=	1,627	928	620	124	306
	%	%	%	%	%
Better	61	56	69	62	67
Worse	20	22	17	23	16
No difference	11	13	9	8	11
No opinion	8	9	5	7	6
	100	100	100	100	100

When asked to give reasons why they think children today get a better — or worse — education than in earlier years, those who have children now in the public schools gave these reasons, which are listed in order of mentions:

1. Wider variety of subjects offered
2. Better facilities/equipment
3. Better teaching methods
4. Better qualified teachers
5. Equal opportunities for all students

When those who say that education today is inferior to that received in earlier years, the reasons offered for this view are:

1. Less discipline
2. Lower education standards and requirements
3. Less interest on the part of students
4. Less interest on the part of teachers
5. Too many irrelevant subjects offered

Detailed and different breakdowns of some of the responses to 1973 poll questions are provided in this section as a supplement to tables already presented.

The Major Problems

What do you think are the biggest problems with which the *public* schools in this community must deal?

	National Totals	No Children In School	Public School Parents	Private School Parents	Professional Educators
N=	1,627 %	928 %	620 %	124 %	306 %
Lack of discipline	22	20	24	32	24
Integration/ segregation	18	22	14	15	19
Lack of proper financial support	16	14	20	10	35
Difficulty in getting "good" teachers	13	9	16	21	8
Use of drugs	10	11	8	12	4
Size of school/classes	9	7	10	17	13
Poor curriculum	7	7	7	10	16
Lack of proper facilities	4	3	5	4	9
Parents' lack of interest	4	4	5	2	11
School board policies	4	4	5	2	5
Pupils' lack of interest	3	4	2	2	9
Communication problems	1	1	1	1	3
Transportation	--	--	--	--	-
There are no problems	4	3	6	2	2
Miscellaneous	4	3	5	3	7
Don't know	13	16	7	8	1

What's Right with the Schools?

In your own opinion, in what ways are your local *public* schools particularly good?

	National Totals	No Children In School	Public School Parents	Private School Parents	Professional Educators
N=	1,627 %	928 %	620 %	124 %	306 %
The curriculum	26	21	34	28	34
The teachers	23	17	32	23	38

(Continued on next page)

School facilities	8	7	9	7	16
Extracurricular activities	7	7	6	5	7
Up-to-date teaching methods	5	5	6	4	15
No racial conflicts	4	4	3	1	5
Good administration	4	3	4	4	8
Small school/ classes	3	3	3	2	8
Good student-teacher relationships	3	3	3	3	3
Equal opportunity for all	3	4	1	4	5
Parental interest/ participation	2	2	3	2	7
Good discipline	2	2	3	3	3
Close to home	1	1	1	1	--
Good lunch program	1	1	2	2	1
Kids are kept off the street	1	1	1	--	1
Transportation system	--	--	--	--	--
Nothing is good	6	5	6	15	4
Miscellaneous	2	1	2	1	2
Don't know	28	37	15	22	4

Changes in Attitudes in Recent Years

The basic table indicating whether public attitudes toward the schools have become more or less favorable appears earlier. The following table provides a different kind of breakdown: by city size and area of the country.

Overall Attitude Toward Schools

	Percent Totals	More Favorable	Less Favorable	No Change	Don't Know
	100 %	32 %	36 %	23 %	9 %
City Size					
500,000 and over	100	28	37	26	9

50,000 to 499,999	100	30	44	20	6
25,000 to 49,999	100	48	27	21	5
Under 25,000	100	33	32	24	11
Area of Country					
East	100	27	37	26	10
Midwest	100	35	34	22	9
South	100	34	35	23	8
West	100	30	41	23	6

The table below indicates sources of school information identified by *those who said their opinions about school quality have changed in recent years*. It supplements the earlier table reporting attitude changes of all respondents.

Attitude Change in Recent Years

	National Totals	More Favor- able	Less Favor- able	No Change	Don't Know
	N= 1,627	515	589	380	143
	%	%	%	%	%
Sources of information					
Newspapers	38	40	38	38	36
Radio and/or television	20	19	24	19	17
Students	43	45	47	41	23
School board/ faculty	33	40	31	33	15
Parents of students	33	35	36	32	23
Other adults in community	23	23	24	22	17
Other	12	13	14	10	6
PTA	3	5	2	3	2
Undesignated	4	2	2	3	20

Are High Schools Getting Too Large?

Responses to the question of ideal size for high schools were reported earlier. A different kind of breakdown is presented below.

Size of Today's Schools

	Percent Totals	Getting Too Large	Not Large Enough	Just Right	Don't Know
	100 %	57 %	13 %	15 %	15 %
City Size					
500,000 and over	100	58	11	14	17
50,000 to 499,999	100	57	12	17	14
25,000 to 49,999	100	56	15	17	12
Under 25,000	100	56	15	14	15

Money Spent Related to Student Achievement

The public's perception of the effects on pupil achievement of different school spending levels was treated earlier. Here is a different kind of breakdown, suggesting that the higher the respondent's education level, the more likely he is to believe that additional money spent on the schools will improve student achievement.

Additional Expenditure of Money Helps

	Percent Totals	Great Deal	Little	None	Don't Know
	100 %	39 %	38 %	10 %	13 %
Education					
Elementary grades	100	24	35	13	28
High school incomplete	100	39	39	12	10
High school complete	100	39	42	9	28
Technical, trade, or business	100	28	43	15	14
College incomplete	100	48	33	8	11
College graduate	100	48	38	5	9

More Emphasis to Career Education

Respondents who agreed that career education should

receive more emphasis in school — and this included 90% of the total (see earlier table) — were asked, "When should this education begin?" Their answers:

	National Totals	No Children In School	Public School Parents	Private School Parents	Professional Educators
N=	1,464	833	561	110	276
	%	%	%	%	%
During elementary school	21	21	21	23	40
During junior and senior high school	76	75	77	77	59
Don't know	3	3	2	--	1
	100	99*	100	100	100

*Due to rounding

Alternative Schools

People in cities of medium size seem particularly favorable to the alternative schools idea:

Establishment of New Kinds of Schools

	Percent Totals	Good Idea	Poor Idea	Don't Know
	100	62	26	12
	%	%	%	%
City Size				
500,000 and over	100	65	22	13
50,000 to 499,999	100	65	26	9
25,000 to 49,999	100	74	14	12
Under 25,000	100	57	30	13

Attitudes Toward School Integration

Responses to the integration question by various categories are shown below. The importance of integration to nonwhite respondents and to the young is apparent. Regional differences appear to be less pronounced than they once were.

School Integration

	Percent Totals	More Should Be Done	Less Should Be Done	No Change	Don't Know
	100 %	**30** %	**38** %	**23** %	**9** %
Sex/race					
Men	100	30	37	25	8
Women	100	30	39	21	10
White	100	26	42	23	9
Nonwhite	100	58	12	23	7
Age					
18 to 20 years	100	46	34	15	5
21 to 29 years	100	42	35	19	4
30 to 49 years	100	31	37	24	8
50 years and older	100	21	42	25	12
Religion					
Protestant	100	27	41	24	8
Roman Catholic	100	34	35	22	9
Jewish	100	35	29	26	10
All others	100	41	32	18	9
Region					
East	100	36	33	22	9
Midwest	100	25	39	27	9
South	100	28	42	20	10
West	100	33	37	22	8
Community size					
500,000 and over	100	37	36	21	6
50,000 to 499,999	100	26	44	23	7
25,000 to 49,999	100	36	27	26	11
Under 25,000	100	26	38	24	12
Education					
Elementary grades	100	24	34	25	17
High school incomplete	100	26	38	26	10
High school complete	100	27	41	22	9
Technical, trade, or business	100	35	46	16	3
College incomplete	100	35	41	19	5
College graduate	100	40	31	24	5
Occupation					
Business and professional	100	35	38	22	5
Clerical and sales	100	33	39	20	7
Farm	100	19	43	28	10
Skilled labor	100	25	42	24	9
Unskilled labor	100	35	31	25	9
Non-labor force	100	23	42	22	13
Undesignated	100	37	31	13	19

Income

$15,000 and over	100	29	40	25	6
$10,000 to $14,999	100	30	40	22	8
$ 7,000 to $ 9,999	100	31	41	21	7
$ 5,000 to $ 6,999	100	32	38	23	7
$ 4,000 to $ 4,999	100	30	33	22	15
$ 3,000 to $ 3,999	100	21	31	31	17
Under $3,000	100	34	37	19	10
Undesignated	100	25	21	21	33

Why Do Families Move to the Suburbs?

The question and a detailed breakdown of the responses follow:

As you know, many families living in the big cities of the nation are moving to the suburbs. Why, in your opinion, are they doing this?

	National Totals	No Children In School	Public School Parents	Private School Parents	Profes- sional Educators
	N= 1,627	928	620	124	306
	%	%	%	%	%
Reasons for Moving					
Big-city conges- tion*	37	37	37	42	23
Fear of high crime level	24	24	23	23	28
Less pollution*	17	16	18	18	14
To get away from minorities	14	14	14	15	29
Better educational opportunities	12	12	12	19	27
More open spaces	11	10	12	10	12
More desirable housing	11	9	13	19	12
Better environ- ment for children	9	8	10	8	8
Cities are too noisy	7	8	6	5	5
High city taxes	6	6	4	9	5
Deterioration of the big cities	4	3	4	7	4

(Continued on next page)

*Combined in summary, page 168.

Lack of privacy	3	4	3	1	1
To create friendships	3	3	2	4	3
Improve one's standard of living	3	3	4	3	7
Lower rental costs	2	2	1	2	1
Lower cost of living in suburbs	2	3	2	1	3
Better employment opportunities	1	1	1	1	2
Children get in more trouble in cities	1	2	1	3	1
Drug problem	1	2	1	2	3
Status symbol	1	1	1	1	5
Miscellaneous	4	4	4	4	8
Don't know	6	6	5	4	--

The Importance of Education to Success

Differential responses by various categories to the question concerning the relation of schooling and success appear below.

		Importance of Schooling			
	Percent Totals	Extremely Important	Fairly Important	Not Too Important	No Opinion
N=	100 %	76 %	19 %	4 %	2 %
Sex/race					
Men	100	72	21	5	2
Women	100	79	18	3	--
White	100	74	20	4	2
Nonwhite	100	84	13	--	2
Age					
18 to 20 years	100	63	34	3	--
21 to 29 years	100	72	22	5	1

30 to 49 years	100	79	18	2	1
50 years and older	100	75	17	5	3
Religion					
Protestant	100	78	18	3	1
Roman Catholic	100	74	21	3	2
Jewish	100	79	18	3	--
All others	100	63	24	8	5
Region					
East	100	74	20	5	1
Midwest	100	76	19	4	1
South	100	78	18	2	2
West	100	74	20	5	1
Community size					
500,000 and over	100	77	19	3	1
50,000 to 499,999	100	75	19	6	--
25,000 to 49,999	100	76	22	1	1
Under 25,000	100	75	20	3	2
Education					
Elementary grades	100	72	20	4	4
High school incomplete	100	73	19	7	1
High school complete	100	81	16	2	1
Technical, trade, or business	100	82	15	2	1
College incomplete	100	71	23	4	2
College graduate	100	71	23	4	2
Occupation					
Business and professional	100	73	22	3	2
Clerical and sales	100	79	16	3	2
Farm	100	77	17	3	3
Skilled labor	100	77	19	3	1
Unskilled labor	100	76	19	4	1
Non-labor force	100	73	20	4	3
Undesignated	100	80	9	7	4
Income					
$15,000 and over	100	75	20	4	1
$10,000 to $14,999	100	79	18	2	1
$7,000 to $9,999	100	76	19	3	2
$5,000 to $6,999	100	78	17	3	2
$4,000 to $4,999	100	70	22	4	4
$3,000 to $3,999	100	77	16	4	3
Under $3,000	100	67	22	5	6
Undesignated	100	71	17	10	2

Is Education Better or Worse Than in Your Day?

Additional breakdowns of the response to a question

concerning the quality of education, past compared with present, appear below.

Today's Education

	Percent Totals	Better	Worse	No Difference	Better/Worse	Don't Know
N=	100	61	20	11	3	5
	%	%	%	%	%	%
Sex/race						
Men	100	60	21	11	2	6
Women	100	61	20	11	4	4
White	100	61	21	11	3	4
Nonwhite	100	59	17	14	3	7
Age						
18 to 20 years	100	57	16	22	1	4
21 to 29 years	100	58	22	11	2	7
30 to 49 years	100	67	18	9	3	3
50 years and older	100	56	23	11	3	7
Religion						
Protestant	100	62	20	10	4	4
Roman Catholic	100	62	20	12	1	5
Jewish	100	53	29	15	--	3
All others	100	52	24	13	2	9
Region						
East	100	59	22	11	2	6
Midwest	100	61	20	13	3	3
South	100	66	17	10	2	5
West	100	54	25	11	3	7
Community size						
500,000 and over	100	56	23	13	2	7
50,000 to 499,999	100	63	21	10	2	4
25,000 to 49,999	100	66	12	10	7	5
Under 25,000	100	62	19	10	3	5
Education						
Elementary grades	100	62	17	10	2	9
High school incomplete	100	57	23	11	3	6
High school complete	100	62	20	12	3	3
Technical, trade, or business	100	56	25	10	2	7
College incomplete	100	62	18	13	3	4
College graduate	100	60	24	10	3	3

Occupation

Business and professional	100	64	17	12	4	3
Clerical and sales	100	63	22	9	3	3
Farm	100	58	23	12	3	4
Skilled labor	100	65	19	10	2	4
Unskilled labor	100	61	20	12	2	5
Non-labor force	100	51	.26	12	2	9

Ways in Which Today's Education Is Better

An earlier table shows that 61% of all respondents thought elementary and secondary school children today get a better education than the respondents themselves did. Asked in what ways the schools are now better, they replied as follows:

	National Totals	No Children In School	Public School Parents	Private School Parents	Professional Educators
N=	1,627	928	620	124	306
	%	%	%	%	%
Better					
Wider variety of subjects offered	33	30	38	35	37
Better facilities/ equipment	21	19	25	19	26
Better qualified teachers	13	13	12	10	21
Up-to-date teaching methods*	11	10	12	15	9
Less structured teaching*	4	4	4	5	14
Equal opportunities for all	3	3	3	2	2
Special help available	1	--	2	2	5
Educational system is better (general)	1	1	1	1	--
Miscellaneous	2	2	3	1	4
Don't know	2	2	2	2	1

*Combined in earlier table as "better teaching methods."

Those who answered that education is worse today gave these reasons:

	National Totals	No Children In School	Public School Parents	Private School Parents	Professional Educators
N=	1,627	928	620	124	306
	%	%	%	%	%
Worse					
Less discipline	7	8	7	5	7
Educational requirements are lower	5	5	4	3	5
Lack of student interest	4	5	3	4	4
Lack of interest by teachers	3	3	3	5	1
Too many irrelevant subjects offered	3	3	3	3	1
Lack of qualified teachers	2	2	3	2	1
Larger school, classes too large	2	3	2	3	3
Too many educational experiments	1	1	1	1	2
Poor student/ teacher relationships	--	--	1	1	--
Educational system is worse (general)	--	--	--	2	-
Miscellaneous	2	2	1	4	3
Don't know	--	1	--	1	1

Analysis of Respondents

National Adults

No children in school	57%
Public school parents	38%*
Parochial and private school parents	8%*

*Totals exceed 43% because some parents have children attending more than one kind of school.

A key element in making comparisons with earlier years is to keep constant the number of persons with *no children in school.* This has been done by a simple weighting process carried out by the computer.

Sex	%
Men	49
Women	51
	100

Race	
White	88
Nonwhite	12
	100

Age	
18-20 years	5
21-29 years	18
30-49 years	40
50 years and over	37
	100

Religion	
Protestant	61
Roman Catholic	27
Jewish	2
Others	10
	100

Region	
East	27
Midwest	28
South	27
West	18
	100

Community size	
500,000 and over	31
50,000 to 499,999	25
25,000 to 49,999	4
Under 25,000	40
	100

Education	
Elementary grades	15
High school incomplete	17
High school complete	33
Technical, trade, or business school	6
College incomplete	16
College graduate	13
	100

(Continued on next page)

Occupation

Business and professional	25
Clerical and sales	10
Farm	4
Skilled labor	20
Unskilled labor	20
Non-labor force	18
Undesignated	3
	100

Income

$15,000 and over	25
$10,000 – $14,999	26
$ 7,000 – $ 9,999	15
$ 5,000 – $ 6,999	13
$ 4,000 – $ 4,999	6
$ 3,000 – $ 3,999	5
Under $2,999	8
Undesignated	2
	100

Design of the Sample

The Gallup Organization, Inc., maintains a national probability sample of interviewing areas that is used for all *Trends* surveys. *Trends* is the Gallup "omnibus" service. For each survey, a minimum of 1,500 individuals are personally interviewed. An independent sample of individuals is selected for each survey.

The sampling procedure is designed to produce an approximation of the adult civilian population, 18 years and older, living in the United States, except for those persons in institutions such as prisons or hospitals.

The design of the sample is that of a replicated probability sample down to the block level in the case of urban areas, and to segments of townships in the case of rural areas. Approximately 300 sampling locations are used in each survey. Interpenetrating samples can be provided for any given study when appropriate.

The sample design included stratification by these four size-of-community strata, using 1970 census data: 1) cities of population 1,000,000 and over; 2) 250,000 to 999,999; 3) 50,000 to 249,999; 4) all other population. Each of these strata was further stratified into seven geographic regions: New England, Middle Atlantic, East Central, West Central, South, Mountain, and Pacific. Within each city size/regional stratum, the population was arrayed in geographic order and zoned into equal-sized groups of sampling units. Pairs of localities were selected in each zone, with probability of selection of each locality proportional to its population size in the 1970 census, producing two replicated samples of localities.

Within localities so selected for which the requisite population data are reported, subdivisions were drawn with the probability of selection proportional to size of population. In all other localities, small definable geographic areas were selected with equal probability.

Separately for each survey, within each subdivision so selected for which block statistics are available, a sample of blocks or block clusters is drawn with probability of selection proportional to the number of dwelling units. In all other subdivisions or areas, blocks or segments are drawn at random or with equal probability.

In each cluster of blocks and each segment so selected, a randomly selected starting point is designated on the interviewer's map of the area. Starting at this point, interviewers are required to follow a given direction in the selection of households until their assignment is completed.

Interviewing is conducted at times when adults, in general, are most likely to be at home, which means on weekends, or if on weekdays, after 4:00 p.m. for women and after 6:00 p.m. for men.

Allowance for persons not at home is made by a "times-at-home" weighting procecure rather than by "call-backs." This procedure is a standard method for reducing the sample bias that would otherwise result from underrepresentation in the sample of persons who are difficult to find at home.

The prestratification by regions is routinely supplemented by fitting each obtained sample to the latest available Census Bureau estimates of the regional distribution of the population. Also minor adjustments of the sample are made by educational attainment ·by men and women separately, based on the annual estimates of the Census Bureau (derived from their Current Population Survey) and by age.

SAMPLING TOLERANCES

In interpreting survey results, it should be borne in mind that all sample surveys are subject to sampling error, that is, the extent to which the results may differ from what would be obtained if the whole population surveyed had been interviewed. The size of such sampling errors depends largely on the number of interviews.

The following tables may be used in estimating the sampling error of any percentage in this report. The computed allowances have taken into account the effect of the sample design upon sampling error. They may be interpreted as indicating the range (plus or minus that figure shown) within which the results of repeated samplings in the same time period could be expected to vary, 95% of the time, assuming the same sampling procedure, the same interviewers, and the same questionnaire.

Table 1 shows how much allowance should be made for the sampling error of a percentage.

The table would be used in the following manner: let us say a reported percentage is 33 for a group which includes 1,500 respondents. Then we go to row "percentages near 30" in the table and go across to the column headed "1,500.' The number at this point is 3, which means that the 33% obtained in the sample is subject to a sampling error of plus or minus 3 points. Another way of saying it is that very probably (95 chances out of 100) the average of repeated samplings would be somewhere between 30 and 36, with the most likely figure the 33 obtained.

In comparing survey results in two samples, such as, for example, men and women, the question arises as to how large must a difference between them be before one can be reasonably sure that it reflects a real difference. In the tables below, the number of points which must be allowed for in such comparisons is indicated.

Two tables are provided. Table 2A is for percentages near 20 or 80; Table 2B is for percentages near 50. For percentages in between, the error to be allowed for is between those shown in the two tables.

Here is an example of how the tables would be used: Let us say that 50% of men respond a certain way and 40% of women respond that way also, for a difference of 10

(Continued on page 188)

Table 1

Recommended Allowance for
Sampling Error of a Percentage

In Percentage Points
(at 95 in 100 confidence level)*

Size of Sample	1,500	1,000	750	600	400	200	100
Percentages near 10	2	2	3	3	4	5	7
Percentages near 20	2	3	4	4	5	7	9
Percentages near 30	3	4	4	4	6	8	10
Percentages near 40	3	4	4	5	6	8	11
Percentages near 50	3	4	4	5	6	8	11
Percentages near 60	3	4	4	5	6	8	11
Percentages near 70	3	4	4	4	6	8	10
Percentages near 80	2	3	4	4	5	7	9
Percentages near 90	2	2	3	3	4	5	7

Table 2A-2B

Recommended Allowance for
Sampling Error of the Difference

In Percentage Points
(at 95 in 100 confidence level)*

Table A — **Percentages near 20 or percentages near 80**

Size of Sample	750	600	400	200
750	5	--	--	--
600	5	6	--	--
400	6	6	7	--
200	8	8	8	10

Table B — **Percentages near 50**

Size of Sample	750	600	400	200
750	6	--	--	--
600	7	7	--	--
400	7	8	8	--
200	10	10	10	12

*The chances are 95 in 100 that the sampling error is not larger than the figures shown.

percentage points between them. Can we say with any assurance that the 10-point difference reflects a real difference between men and women on the question? The sample contains approximately 750 men and 750 women.

Since the percentages are near 50, we consult Table 2B, and since the two samples are about 750 persons each, we look for the number in the column headed "750" which is also in the row designated "750." We find the number 6 here. This means that the allowance for error should be 6 points, and that in concluding that the percentage among men is somewhere between 4 and 16 points higher than the percentage among women we should be wrong only about 5% of the time. In other words, we can conclude with considerable confidence that a difference exists in the direction observed and that it amounts to at least 4 percentage points.

If, in another case, men's responses amount to 22%, say, and women's 24%, we consult Table 2A because these percentages are near 20. We look in the column headed "750" and see that the number is 5. Obviously, then, the two-point difference is inconclusive.

Chapter 7
A Look into Your School District

Why Survey?

In the public school systems of America, professional personnel are responsible to citizens; boards of education are established to reflect the desires of the public. Therefore, school boards and superintendents need systems to assess community desires, attitudes, and knowledge about the educational process and schooling.

Scientific sampling of public opinion is a means of learning how citizens judge the quality of their schools and the criteria they use in determining the excellence or lack of it in their local school system. Opinion surveys permit investigation of specific educational issues, e.g., community attitudes toward school finances, the professional staff, and school board; acceptability of educational innovations; and public awareness of school problems.

The results will permit decision making which is not influenced by pressure groups, telephone feedback, and random discussions — all of which frequently provide faulty conclusions. If surveys are done periodically, with some basic questions repeated, shifts in public opinion and knowledge can be gauged.

This chapter outlines a process your school district can use to determine local public opinion about schools and education. It provides, in a very simple way, a guide to the kinds of information needed. Many books, to which the reader can refer for additional details, have been written on research procedures.

National Comparisons Available

The annual Gallup Polls on the Public's Attitudes Toward the Public Schools, reprinted in this volume, provide a bank of more than 100 questions and results. These results do not apply to any single community; they provide a norm for comparison. Questions and results are not copyrighted and no limitations are placed upon the use of information contained in this volume beyond customary credit to source, accuracy, completeness of quotation, etc. Each annual report includes a description of the research procedures and an analysis of results. (For space reasons, the description of research procedures appears only in Chapter 6 of this volume.)

Subsequent annual polls will be readily available and will be announced each fall in leading educational journals.

Two Prohibitions. While questions and results of each annual survey are available for school district use, users do not have permission to use in any form the name of "Gallup," "Gallup International," "Gallup Poll," etc., nor the name "CFK Ltd."

Selection of Survey Questions

From the bank of questions used in the annual Gallup surveys, select those on which information is desired in your district. Probably you'd like to ask every question available. Don't! You will overtax your interviewers and respondents — and have so much data to tabulate and analyze that detail may obscure the total picture. A 30-minute (or less) interview is what you should strive for. The way to determine the length of an interview is to try the questionnaire on one respondent at a time, paring your list of questions until an average interviewer and respondent take no more than half an hour to go through the entire procedure, including the "demographic" (population statistics) questions. You may want to include questions which have not appeared in the annual national surveys. All questions must be carefully and impartially worded, a task demanding great skill. The following books can provide guidance.

Goode and Hatt, *Methods in Social Research.*

Payne, *The Art of Asking Questions.*

Riley, *Sociological Research: A Case Approach.*

Selltiz, Jahoda, Deutsch, Cook, *Research Methods in Social Relations.*

To cut coding and tabulation time, we strongly urge you to use the minimum of "open" questions. For example, in the 1970 Gallup survey, only one "open" question was used.

Design of the Questionnaire

Here is a reproduction of the first page of a typical survey.

Hello, I'm from the ————————— public schools. I would like to talk with you about the schools in your community.

1. As you know, in some communities there are three kinds of schools — the public schools, the parochial (or church-related) schools, and the private schools (sometimes called "independent" schools).

a. First, I'd like to know if you, yourself, have any children in the local *public* schools?

☐ Yes, how many. . . . .☐ No

b. *Parochial* or *Private* schools?

☐ Yes, how many. . . . .☐ No

2. What do you think are the biggest problems with which the *public* schools in this community must deal?

3. How much do you know about the goals of your local public schools: quite a lot, not very much, almost nothing?

☐ Quite a lot   ☐ Not very much   ☐ Almost nothing

We suggest that the interviewer use the opening lines to identify himself and the purpose of the visit. The first question provides needed information and sets the stage easily.

Now, place the selected survey questions in appropriate order. Place questions so that any one question or response does not suggest a response for a subsequent item. For example, in the following list the second two questions could suggest answers for the first question, an undesirable situation.

— What do you think are the biggest problems with which the public schools in this community must deal?

— How do you feel about the discipline in the local schools — is it too strict, not strict enough, or just about right?

— Some people feel the schools do not go far enough in regulating the way boys and girls dress for school. Do you think there should be greater regulation of the way children dress for school, or less?

Before your questionnaire is printed, ask the person who will handle the data processing to properly "pre-code" the "closed" questions (those with answer boxes). Your final questions provide the demographic data. Any or all can be omitted, depending upon the desired degrees of stratification of the results. Those following correspond to the Gallup surveys:

And now, finally, just a few questions about yourself so that we can be sure we have an accurate cross-section of the public.

Could you tell me the kind of business or industry the *chief wage earner (head of household)* in your immediate family works in and the kind of work he does there?

Kind of business _____

Kind of work _____

What was the last grade or class you COMPLETED in school?

☐ Elementary   ☐ Technical, trade, or business
☐ H.S. Incomplete   school
☐ H.S. Graduate   ☐ College, univ. incomplete
         ☐ College, univ. graduate

And what is your age, please? _____

What is your religious preference — Protestant, Roman Catholic, Jewish, or other?

☐ Protestant ☐ Roman Catholic ☐ Jewish
☐ Other ☐ None

(*Show Hand-out Card.*) Would you please give me the letter of the group which best represents the total annual income, before taxes, of all of the members of your immediate family living in your household?

☐ A ☐ B ☐ C ☐ D ☐ E ☐ F ☐ G ☐ H

Check Whether:

☐ White man   ☐ Nonwhite man
☐ White woman   ☐ Nonwhite woman

Determining the Survey Sample

In sampling terms, the whole is the "universe" — the total population of the school district. The survey director must use a method whereby a representative "sample" (group of citizens), which will represent all elements in the same proportion as they are present in the whole, can be selected from the "universe." For your purposes, the important elements are sex, race, age, occupation, education, economic status, and religious preference. When sampling is performed so that every adult in the school district's population has an equal chance of being selected, the errors of sampling are satisfactorily controlled. The sample approach is a reliable process for selecting respondents within predetermined limits of precision.

"Drawing a sample" requires specific statistical training and skill. We suggest asking the head of the sociology department or school of education at your nearest college to recommend a member of his staff who is qualified.

Maps of the individual areas for interviewing assignments are as important as the process of selecting these areas. The following criteria should be used:

— The maps must show the most recent subdivisions and indicate in detail such features as roads, boundaries of towns, townships, and counties, as well as natural features such as brooks, lakes, and rivers.

— The maps should be black and white so that they can be easily marked and copied, and they should be sufficiently detailed for easy reading.

Such maps are usually available at the city or county engineer's office.

A map reproduction of the assigned area should be prepared for each interviewer. Lines are marked in red ink to indicate the boundaries of the interviewing area; an "x" should be marked to indicate the point at which the interviewer should begin the interview.

Your sampling adviser will tell you how interviewers should select homes, and individuals within each home, for interviews.

Recruitment of Interviewers

At the crux of the data gathering are the interviewers who objectively gather opinions and facts on questionnaires from people in their assigned areas. Parent organizations, A.A.U.W., Jaycees, and other groups of concerned citizens are prime sources of volunteer interviewers. In recruiting, try to obtain a large cross-section of citizens; this helps to prevent a bias in influencing responses to questions. Explain that the assignment will take about 10 hours of each person's time, including a training session to be held on (date). Your sampling adviser will tell you how many interviewers you need. Recruit about 20% more, so that there are substitutes in case of illness or other reasons for some not following through on their assignments.

Training Interviewers

The major tasks to be accomplished during the session are:

1. Persuade interviewers of the importance of the survey and of doing the interviewing to the best of their ability.

2. Emphasize the importance of remaining neutral as the interview is being conducted. This is an absolute mandatory stance on the part of the interviewer.

3. Teach them how to interview. Have them "pair off." Distribute one questionnaire to each pair. Tell them that one in each pair will interview the other. Give them these general rules:

— Read all questions exactly as they are worded. Each

word has been included to serve a certain purpose. Changing any word or phrase can alter significantly the meaning of a question and therefore can completely destroy the purpose and usefulness of that question.

— Use number 2 pencils to record responses; these provide the most easily read markings for those who will code and tabulate.

— Use a clipboard or magazine under the questionnaire to provide a firm writing surface.

Now have them start the interviews. As problems emerge, a member of the Survey Director's Committee should handle them for that pair. If he thinks it a vital problem, he may stop the entire group, explain the problem and its importance, and suggest how it be handled. Or he may decide to wait until these interviews are completed and then discuss all problems that emerged and his suggestions for handling them.

The questionnaires are collected and new questionnaires distributed, one to each pair. Now the other person becomes the interviewer.

What have you accomplished? All interviewers are now familiar with the questionnaire, the hand-out cards, the procedures — and hopefully, they've had fun learning.

Close the meeting by telling them when and where they will get their assignments and the importance of following all instructions they receive.

Finally, distribute a printed form telling:

— When and where they will get their assignments (yes, they will forget your verbal instructions).

— The dates and hours of interviewing.

— What to do if they cannot fulfill their commitment.

— When and where they should return the completed questionnaires.

(In using volunteer interviewers you may have to provide baby-sitter services during your training session.)

Interviewing Assignments

Start interviewing within a day or two after the training session. The interviewers are excited and interested at this point; if time lags between training and interviewing, interest will be lost and instructions forgotten. Schedule interviewing time for weekday evenings or anytime on weekends, depending on what is best in your community. In this way everyone has an equal chance of being interviewed, whether he works or not.

Assign a team leader for every 10 interviewers. He assumes responsibility for putting together, picking up, and delivering materials, plus filling in as an interviewer if the need arises.

The envelope in which material will be delivered and returned should contain:

— Instruction sheet
— Identification button or card
— Questionnaires
— Hand-out cards
— Assignment sheets
— Maps

Assign no more than five or six interviews to each volunteer. (Your sampling adviser will have guided you in assigning interviewing locations and quota of interviews for each interviewer.)

We recommend an interviewer not be assigned streets on which he is known, so that respondents will feel more free to express themselves.

It is important to keep good records of which interviewers are assigned to which areas — who still has materials — who has returned materials — who has completed his assignment — who has not.

Processing the Results

The reduction of thousands of questions to a relatively few pages of statistical tables takes three steps:

— *Coding Responses.* To deal with the numerous individual responses for "open" questions, establish a coding system so that replies of the same nature can be grouped into categories. Each category is assigned a number. After carefully reading each response, the "coder" assigns the appropriate number in the margin of the questionnaire. A miscellaneous category covers answers too few to warrant a separate category. Codes for Gallup "open" questions appear in the previous chapters.

"Closed" questions have been precoded before printing,

as suggested in "Design of the Questionnaire."

— *Transferring Data.* Coded responses for each question and the demographic data are then transferred to keypunch cards by the data processing organization. All data is then in a form easily counted and analyzed.

— *Counting and Sorting.* The example below illustrates what can be done with information after key-punching.

Q. Do you think teachers should have the right to strike?

☐ Yes   ☐ No   ☐ No opinion

The machine counts the answers

Yes	179
No	206
No opinion	12
Total	397

Results should be tabulated in percentages. Depending on the demographic questions asked, you may get data stratified in many ways. Following are those which correspond to the Gallup reports.

Adults
>No children in schools
>Public school parents
>Parochial and private school parents

Occupation
>Business and professional
>Clerical and sales
>Farm
>Skilled labor
>Unskilled labor
>Non-labor force
>Undesignated

Education
>Elementary grades
>High school incomplete
>High school graduate
>Technical, trade, or business school
>College incomplete
>College graduate
>Undesignated

Sex
   Men
   Women

Age
   Under 21 years
   21 to 29 years
   30 to 49 years
   50 years and over

Race
   White
   Nonwhite

Religion
   Protestant
   Roman Catholic
   Jewish
   Other

Income (This is the material that appears on the hand-out card. See "Design of the Questionnaire.")
   $15,000 and over
   $10,000 to $14,999
   $ 7,000 to $ 9,999
   $ 5,000 to $ 6,999
   $ 3,000 to $ 4,999
   Under $2,999
   Undesignated

High School Juniors and Seniors (If included in survey)

Public school	Under 15 years
Parochial school	16 years
Private school	17 years
	18 years
	19 years and over

Summarizing the Findings

The Gallup reports in the preceding chapters provide ideas and processes which might be used to report your results. Each report contains sections describing the purpose of the study, the research procedure, observations and conclusions, statistical data for each question, and composition of the sample. In addition, your sampling authority should provide you with sections on design of the sample and sampling tolerances.

Some Concluding Comments

While the school district's public opinion poll provides a greater understanding of public attitudes, it provides a general picture, not a precise one.

Do not attempt to use the concepts and processes described in this chapter to predict the results of a forthcoming school election. A different set of procedures must be used for that purpose and they are not described in this chapter.

We wish you great success with your local poll.

Index